Annette Tison and Talus Taylor

The Big Book of
AMAZING
Animal Behavior

GROSSET & DUNLAP · New York

Originally published and produced by Arnoldo Mondadori S.p.A. Milano
Copyright © 1986, © 1987 by Annette Tison & Talus Taylor. All rights reserved.

First published in the United States of America in 1987
by Grosset & Dunlap, a member of The Putnam Publishing
Group, New York
Published simultaneously in Canada
All rights reserved
Library of Congress Catalog Card Number 86-82561
ISBN 0-448-18998-4

English text editor Jenny Vaughan
English text consultant Michael Boorer

Printed and bound in Spain by Artes Gráficas Toledo S.A.
D. L. TO:1865-1986
A B C D E F G H I J

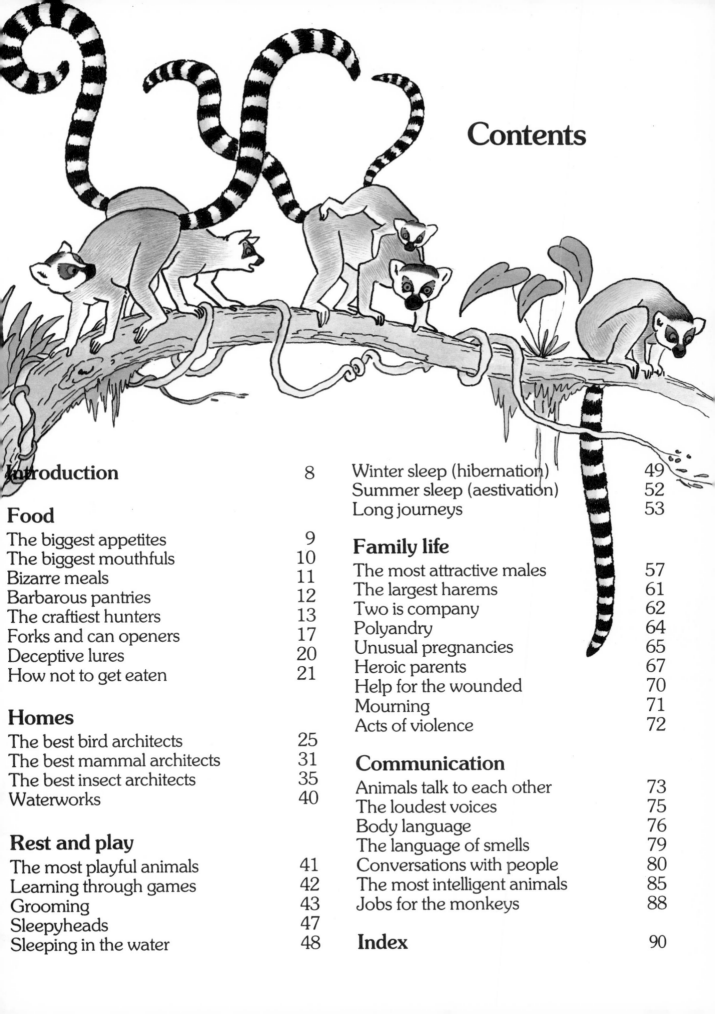

Contents

Introduction

In our first book, *The Big Book of Animal Records*, we looked at what we call the *physical characteristics* of living creatures. These are such things as their size and weight, and the different skills they have.

This book is very similar. It is set out in the same way, using examples of record-breakers as well as interesting facts and anecdotes about animals. It looks at their different lifestyles — how they sleep, eat, build their homes and, most importantly, how they try to make sure their species continues to survive. The way in which each kind of animal does this is not really important. What matters is that it is successful.

Studying animal behavior is a science, and that is what this book is about. It describes some of the latest discoveries about animals and the ways in which they behave. We can learn that perhaps we humans are not, after all, really as special as we might think. We always assume we are the most intelligent of all the animals — but we have plenty of competition!

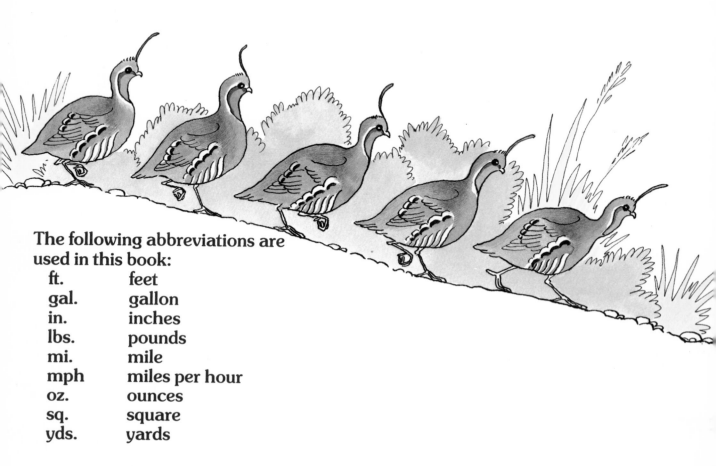

The following abbreviations are used in this book:

ft.	feet
gal.	gallon
in.	inches
lbs.	pounds
mi.	mile
mph	miles per hour
oz.	ounces
sq.	square
yds.	yards

Food

Getting enough to eat isn't as easy as you might think. After all, you can't fill your stomach just by walking around with your mouth open – especially if you're small and not very quick.

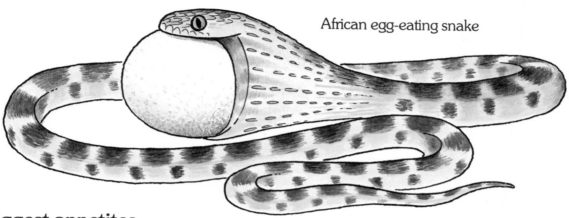

African egg-eating snake

The biggest appetites

Not surprisingly, the largest animals are the ones that eat the most. But curiously, the animals that eat the most in relation to their size are among the tiniest of all.

The blue whale measures up to 100 ft. long and may weigh 143 tons. It absorbs 800 lbs. of plankton (tiny ocean-living creatures) each day. This is an absolute record!

The African elephant, which weighs up to 7 tons, holds the record among herbivorous (plant-eating) animals. It spends between eighteen and twenty hours each day getting through 770 lbs. of vegetation and drinking 24 gal. of water.

The sea elephant holds the record among carnivores (meat- or fish-eaters). It eats 440 lbs. of fish a day.

The pygmy shrew is the hungriest mammal. It is a tiny insectivore (insect-eater) that weighs only $1/10$ oz. Every day it consumes three or four times its own weight in food. It eats frequently, day and night, and will die within two to three hours if it has no food. If you ate as much in proportion to your size, you would eat 2 pigs, 30 chickens, 300 eggs, 50 pears, 3 pineapples and 20 bars of chocolate every day.

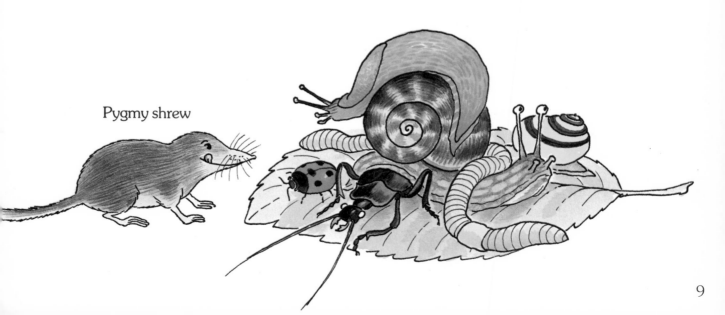

Pygmy shrew

The biggest mouthfuls

Some snakes – such as the African egg-eating snake – can swallow prey two or three times as wide as themselves. They can do this because they have special jaws, without hinges fastening them together.

The reticulated python, up to 33 ft. long, has the record for the biggest mouthful on land. This snake can swallow a whole animal weighing as much as 121 lbs. A whole leopard was once found in a python's stomach!

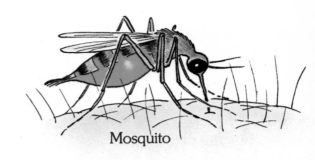
Mosquito

But even the mammals with the biggest appetites cannot compare with insects. A female mosquito will suck the equivalent of her own weight in blood into her body every time she bites you. She can do this fifteen times a day!

Reticulated python

Horned frog

Although snakes can eat so much in one meal, they do not really have big appetites. They may not eat any more than their own weight in a year and can go for a very long time without eating. A poisonous snake called the Okinawa habu once went without food for three years and three months.

The aggressive horned frog can easily eat prey such as mice and lizards, which are the same size as itself.

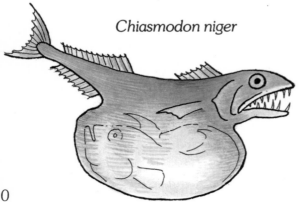
Chiasmodon niger

Many deep-sea fish are known only by their Latin names as they have no common ones. The *Chiasmodon niger* has a stomach that expands so that it can swallow prey bigger than itself.

zarre meals

ting people

ere are sensational stories about wild animals eating
ople. Many were invented by hunters as an excuse to kill
imals, but there are creatures that eat humans if they get the
ance. Among these are the great white shark, the piranha
n and, most notoriously, the saltwater crocodile, which may
responsible for the deaths of up to 2000 people a year.
ccasionally a leopard, lion or tiger will become a man-eater.

Tear drinking moths

Mosquitoes, fleas and lice are far more
common and much smaller – but they still
enjoy eating parts of humans, such as blood
or skin.

Tear drinkers
A moth in Thailand feeds on the lachrymal
fluid (tears) of oxen.

Darwin's finch

Blue-footed booby

Blood suckers
Darwin's finches are found in the Galapa-
gos Islands. One has developed the habit of
pecking seabirds' feathers and sucking the
drops of blood that appear when it has done
this. The picture shows one at work on a
blue-footed booby. The oxpeckers of Africa
have a similar unpleasant habit. They peck
through the hides of animals such as buffalo.

Barbarous pantries

Many animals take the wise precaution of storing up food "for a rainy day." Squirrels, for example, store nuts to eat in the winter, and other rodents behave in similar ways.

Red-backed shrike

Many of us have seen how dogs bury bones and come back for them later. Here are some examples of other animals that make food stores — in some rather nasty ways.

The red-backed shrike impales its prey on the thorns of bushes near its nest. While we are sad for the mice, insects and frogs the shrike has caught, we should not think the bird is cruel. The shrike needs these creatures as food for its babies. Many other birds eat mice, but mice sometimes eat birds, so perhaps things even out after all.

The common mole eats worms. It paralyzes them by biting their heads, and then stores them away. Its underground store can hold up to 1000 of these mutilated worms. The mole needs them all, for itself and its young. Without its storeroom, the mole and its young would die in a few hours.

Common mole

Honeypot ant

Honeypot ants have a most unusual way of storing food. They use each other as living honeypots. Their stomachs become enormously stretched, so full of honey that they are almost bursting. They cling to the ceiling of their chamber, like lanterns. When food is scarce, the contents of their stomachs are regurgitated (brought back up) into the mouths of other worker ants.

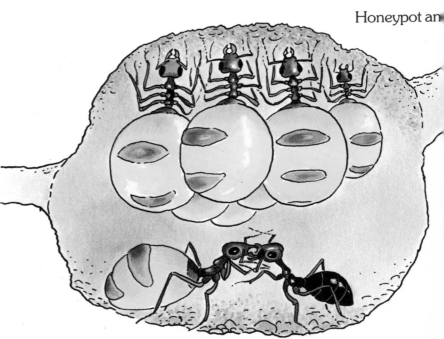

The craftiest hunters

Grass- and leaf-eating animals do not have to run after their meals, but the situation is quite different for flesh-eating animals. Their food can run and fly – it is very easy for it to escape. Hunters need speed, strength, patience and cunning. Trap building is the peak of the art of hunting – and some spiders are the experts.

Nephila spider's web

The biggest spider's web is made by a tropical spider of the *Nephila* family. Its web is 6 ft. across. The supporting threads can be 20 ft. long. People in Papua, New Guinea use these threads for fishing lines, while in Madagascar they are woven into cloth. Each spider can produce 460 ft. of silk in 1¼ hours.

The simplest web is made by the stick spider. It is just a single sticky thread about 9 in. long.

The largest collective webs are made by spiders in the *Stegodyphus* family. These webs can cover all the vegetation, including trees, for several miles.

The only mammal to use traps (apart from humans) is the humpback whale. Using its blowhole, it makes a network of bubbles that forms a cylinder. Plankton are caught in this net. The whale rises up at the center of this trap with its mouth open and swallows the plankton.

Humpback whale

Bubbles

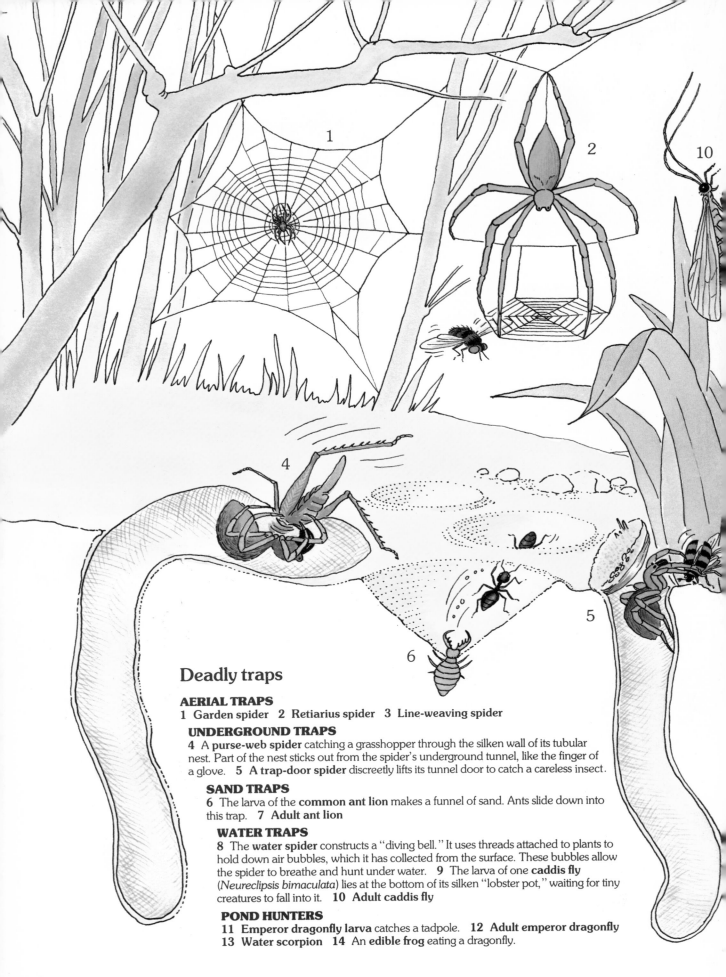

Deadly traps

AERIAL TRAPS
1 Garden spider   2 Retiarius spider   3 Line-weaving spider

UNDERGROUND TRAPS
4 A **purse-web spider** catching a grasshopper through the silken wall of its tubular nest. Part of the nest sticks out from the spider's underground tunnel, like the finger of a glove.   5 A **trap-door spider** discreetly lifts its tunnel door to catch a careless insect.

SAND TRAPS
6 The larva of the **common ant lion** makes a funnel of sand. Ants slide down into this trap.   7 **Adult ant lion**

WATER TRAPS
8 The **water spider** constructs a "diving bell." It uses threads attached to plants to hold down air bubbles, which it has collected from the surface. These bubbles allow the spider to breathe and hunt under water.   9 The larva of one **caddis fly** (*Neureclipsis bimaculata*) lies at the bottom of its silken "lobster pot," waiting for tiny creatures to fall into it.   10 **Adult caddis fly**

POND HUNTERS
11 **Emperor dragonfly larva** catches a tadpole.   12 **Adult emperor dragonfly**
13 **Water scorpion**   14 An **edible frog** eating a dragonfly.

7

3

12

14

8

11

9

13

15

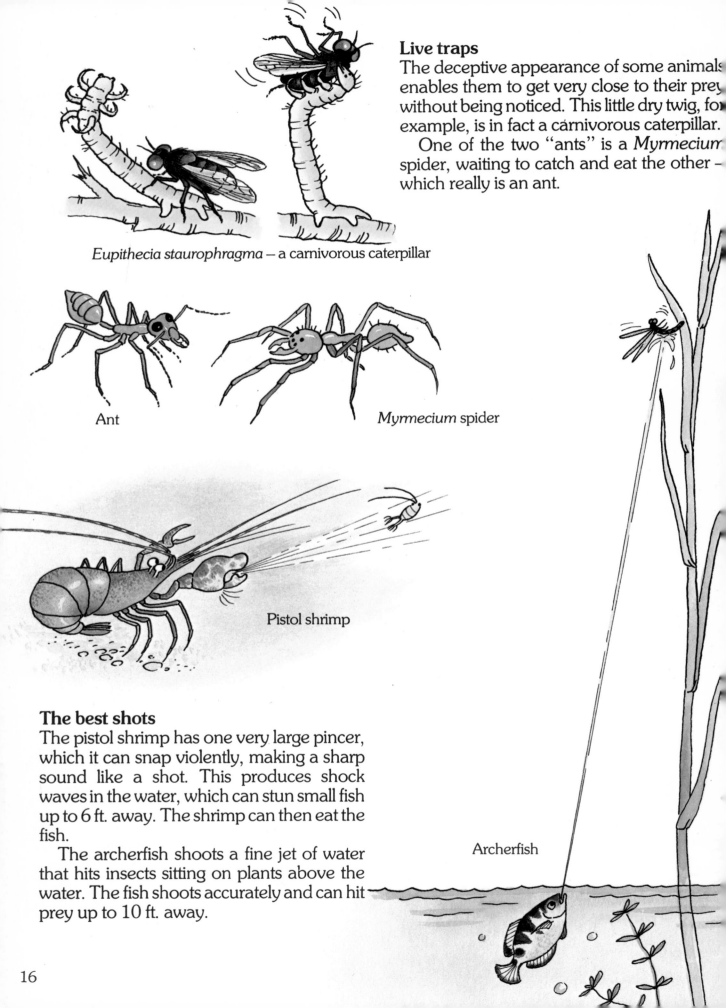

Live traps

The deceptive appearance of some animals enables them to get very close to their prey without being noticed. This little dry twig, for example, is in fact a carnivorous caterpillar.

One of the two "ants" is a *Myrmecium* spider, waiting to catch and eat the other – which really is an ant.

Eupithecia staurophragma – a carnivorous caterpillar

Ant

Myrmecium spider

Pistol shrimp

The best shots

The pistol shrimp has one very large pincer, which it can snap violently, making a sharp sound like a shot. This produces shock waves in the water, which can stun small fish up to 6 ft. away. The shrimp can then eat the fish.

The archerfish shoots a fine jet of water that hits insects sitting on plants above the water. The fish shoots accurately and can hit prey up to 10 ft. away.

Archerfish

Forks and can-openers

People used to think that one of the reasons we could say that humans were superior to other animals was that we can use tools. Now we know that there are plenty of other creatures that can do this. Mammals, birds and even some insects can use tools of various kinds. So perhaps we humans are not so superior after all! Described and illustrated on this page are a few examples of tools that are used by animals.

The chimpanzee uses a carefully chosen twig to dip into the entrance of a termite's nest. When the stick comes out, it is covered with termites, which the chimpanzee licks off. Then it puts the twig back in the nest. It looks easy, but people who have tried to copy the trick had no luck. Not all twigs will work, and they have to be jiggled in a special way.

Chimpanzees

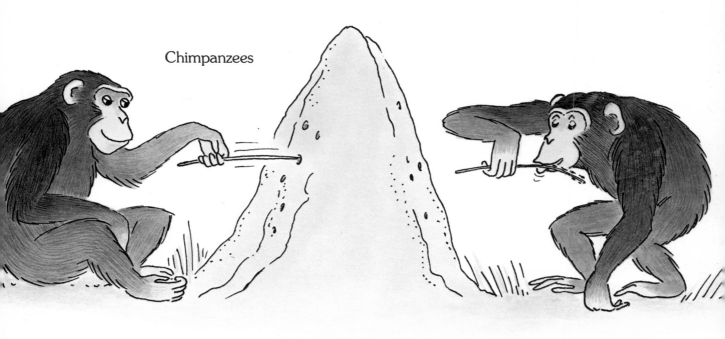

Woodpecker finch

The beak of the woodpecker finch is not as long as that of a real woodpecker. The finch makes up for this by using a cactus thorn to extract insects hiding under the bark of trees or in cracks in the wood. We do not know if people have ever tried to copy this trick, but the finch would certainly beat humans in any insect-catching competition. After all, the finch has had a lot more practice.

17

An exhibition of can-openers

1 The **sea otter** uses a pebble to get a mollusk (shellfish) out of its shell. It swims on its back, holding a flat stone on its belly. It hammers the shell against this stone.   **2** The **song thrush** breaks the shell of a snail by knocking it against a stone.   **3** **Egyptian vultures** hold stones in their beaks and use them to crack open the tough shells of ostrich eggs.   **4** **Polar bears** throw pieces of ice at seals – and not for fun, either!   **5** **Herring gulls** break shells by dropping them on to rocks.
6 Two American pilots, lost for ten months off the coast of Canada, were able to survive by eating seabirds' eggs and shellfish dropped by gulls.   **7** The **robber crab** uses its powerful pincers to cut coconuts from tall trees. Then it goes down to the ground to finish the job of opening them.
8 The **lammergeier** carries off bones from corpses and smashes them open by dropping them on to rocks from a great height, so it can feed on the marrow. It is said to do the same with tortoises, if it can find them.   **9** Legend has it that the Greek poet **Aeschylus** was killed by a tortoise falling on to his bald head.

Deceptive lures

Fishermen are often very proud of the pretty feather lures they make and use. But humans did not invent this way of fishing, for the same method can be observed in many animals. Once again, we have to think about what we mean by "intelligence."

The green heron has been seen carefully placing a small feather on the water's surface when it wants to attract an obstinate fish. The fish comes closer, curious to see if the feather can be eaten, and the clever heron catches it and eats it at once.

Green heron

The assassin bug is found in Costa Rica. It shakes the body of a dead termite at the entrance of a termites' nest. Another termite comes out and tries to grab this lure—and the assassin bug seizes it and eats it. One bug once caught 31 termites in three hours in this way.

Assassin bug

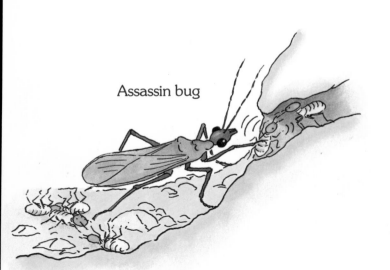

This zoo gibbon used to catch the ducks that swam around its island. It used cookie crumbs to attract them and, when they were close enough, grabbed them, plucked them neatly and ate them.

Gibbon

How not to get eaten

Champions of camouflage

To stay alive, it's not enough just to find food. You have to make sure you do not become part of a meal yourself. The dead-leaf butterfly avoids its enemies by looking just like a dead leaf. There are other insects that look like thorns or twigs — some of them are almost perfect look-alikes.

Still others disguise themselves. The caterpillar of the looper moth cuts bits of petals from the plants on which it lives. It sticks these onto its back. The next two pages show how some sea animals camouflage themselves in similar ways.

False bullies

Some animals frighten their enemies by looking like a more dangerous relative. This harmless scarlet king snake protects itself by mimicking (looking like) the deadly North American coral snake.

Looper moth caterpillar

Dead-leaf butterfly

Scarlet king snake

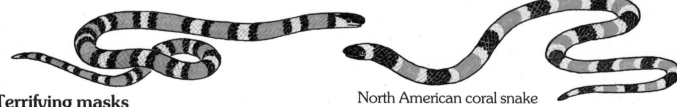

North American coral snake

Terrifying masks

These harmless caterpillars have false "eye" patterns behind their heads. These frighten off their enemies, the birds. The caterpillars' real heads are the little bumps in front of the masks. Some kinds of butterflies also have "eye" patterns on them.

Caterpillars with false "eyes"

North American *Pleurodema bibrioni* frog

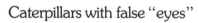

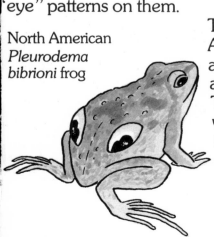

There is a frog in North America that defends itself in a similar way. It is called *Pleurodema bibrioni* and has two small swellings on its back. These look like huge eyes, and when the frog feels threatened, it displays them. This mask may frighten an enemy away.

Sea camouflages

Look carefully! Some of these animals are so well hidden that you will not see them right away.

1 The **striped shrimpfish** hides among the spines of a sea urchin. **2** The **slender pipefish** looks like a ribbon of seaweed.
3 The **green shrimp** lies on seaweed that is exactly the same color as itself.
4 A fearsome dragon and a wonder of mimicry, the **leafy seahorse** can hardly be seen among the sea plants. **5** The **sponge crab** hides under a sponge. It cuts this to size and puts it on its back. The sponge grows at the same rate as the crab.

6 The **spider crab** tears off pieces of seaweed and arranges them on its rough shell. The seaweed stays there, camouflaging the crab. If its surroundings change, the crab puts on different clothes. **7** The **hermit crab** first chooses a shell to live in and then decorates it with bits of sponge and sea anemones. These devices all help to make it fit into its surroundings.

An inflated fish

When frightened, the porcupine fish inflates itself with water. It doubles in size, and its spines stand out; nothing, not even a shark, can eat it.

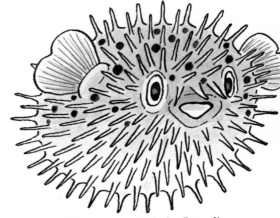

Porcupine fish

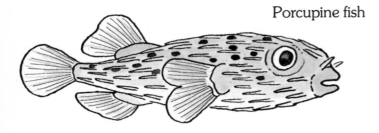

Porcupine fish (inflated)

A talented actor

To deceive an enemy, the North American opossum lies motionless, with its eyes glassy and its tongue hanging out, pretending to be dead. When its enemy has gone, the opossum runs off.

Defensive weapons

When they are threatened, octopuses and squids squirt out a cloud of ink that hides them from their enemies.

The sea cucumber ejects long, sticky threads, called *Cuvieran tubules*. These swell in the water and entangle the attacker.

One crab uses its pincers to pick up small poisonous sea anemones and uses these to threaten enemies.

North American opossum

Common octopus

Moray eel

Crab

Sea-cucumber

Homes

Humans are not the only creatures on this planet that are skilled in various crafts.

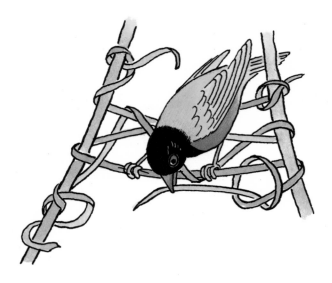

The biggest nest is made by Freycinet's moundbird. This Australian bird is about the size of a partridge. It builds a mound of earth mixed with vegetation up to 16 ft. high and 39 ft. across, which works as an incubator. The bird lays its eggs, one by one, inside the mound. The vegetable matter rots, warming up the mound to about 91°F., the tempera-ture the eggs need to hatch. The bird regularly tests the temperature inside the mound by sticking its open beak into it.

The newly hatched chicks have to struggle for hours to get to the surface and some may suffocate on the way. After that, the chicks must look after themselves, as their parents take no more notice of them.

Freycinet's moundbird

The mound

The most tireless worker is the mallee fowl. It is related to the moundbird. Like its cousin, it builds a mound – though a smaller one – to incubate its eggs. The mound is about 16 ft. across, and the bird looks after it for eleven months of the year. It uses a layer of sand to insulate the nest, and it has to change the thickness of the layer every day. It does this to raise or lower the temperature of the eggs, depending on how warm it is outside. Once the eggs have hatched, the bird can finally take a month's holiday.

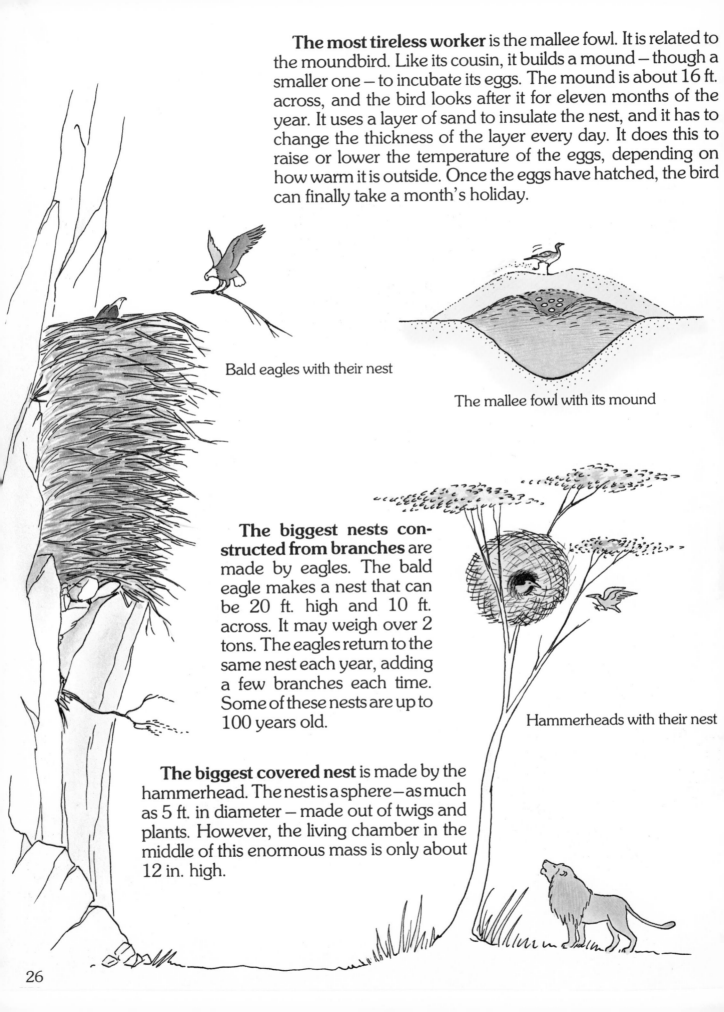

Bald eagles with their nest

The mallee fowl with its mound

The biggest nests constructed from branches are made by eagles. The bald eagle makes a nest that can be 20 ft. high and 10 ft. across. It may weigh over 2 tons. The eagles return to the same nest each year, adding a few branches each time. Some of these nests are up to 100 years old.

Hammerheads with their nest

The biggest covered nest is made by the hammerhead. The nest is a sphere – as much as 5 ft. in diameter – made out of twigs and plants. However, the living chamber in the middle of this enormous mass is only about 12 in. high.

Remarkable structures

Birds build their structures using all sorts of different techniques.

The tailor bird finds a big leaf, rolls it into a cone and sews the edges together.

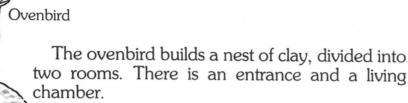
Ovenbird

The tailor bird with its nest

The ovenbird builds a nest of clay, divided into two rooms. There is an entrance and a living chamber.

—Entrance

Living chamber

The carpenters

Many birds make their nests in hollow trees, but only the woodpecker can actually hollow out a solid tree with its beak to make a nest hole. It usually uses the same nest for several years in a row, unless another bird, such as a nuthatch, steals it. Notice how the nuthatch has used mud to make the nest's entrance narrower so that the woodpecker cannot get its home back.

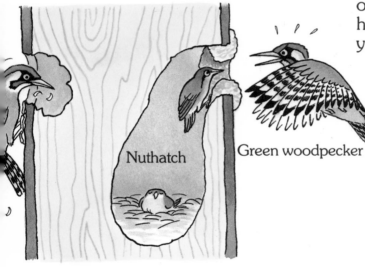
Nuthatch

Green woodpecker

Kingfisher

Weaverbird

Diggers and weavers

The kingfisher digs out a long tunnel in the bank of a river and builds its nest at the end.

Many birds make nests by weaving grass, cotton, twigs and other suitable materials. The weaverbirds are the champions at doing this.

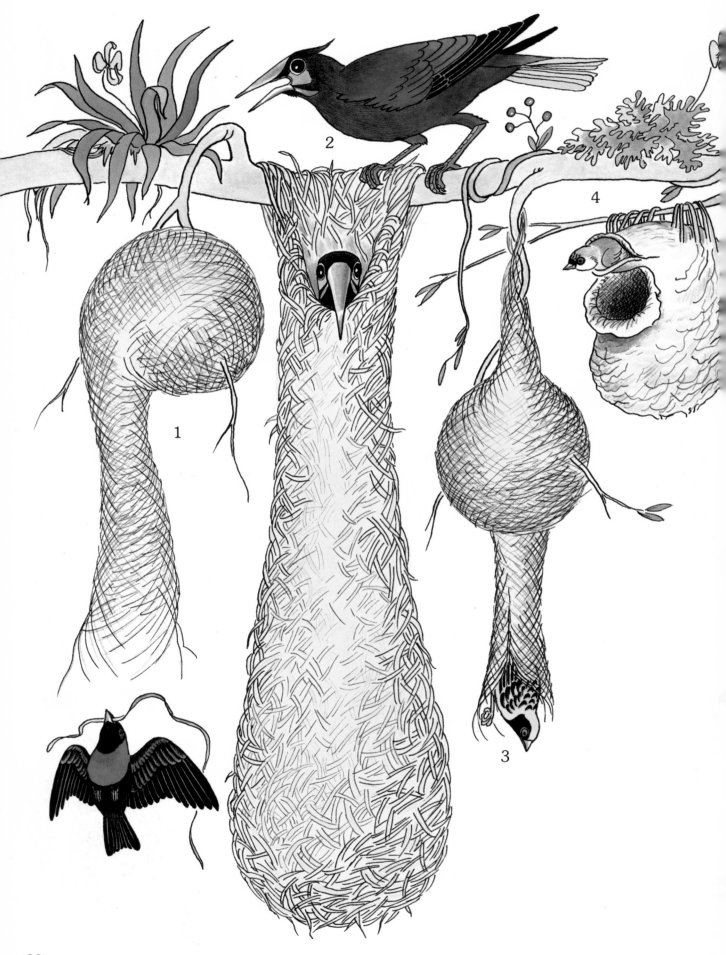

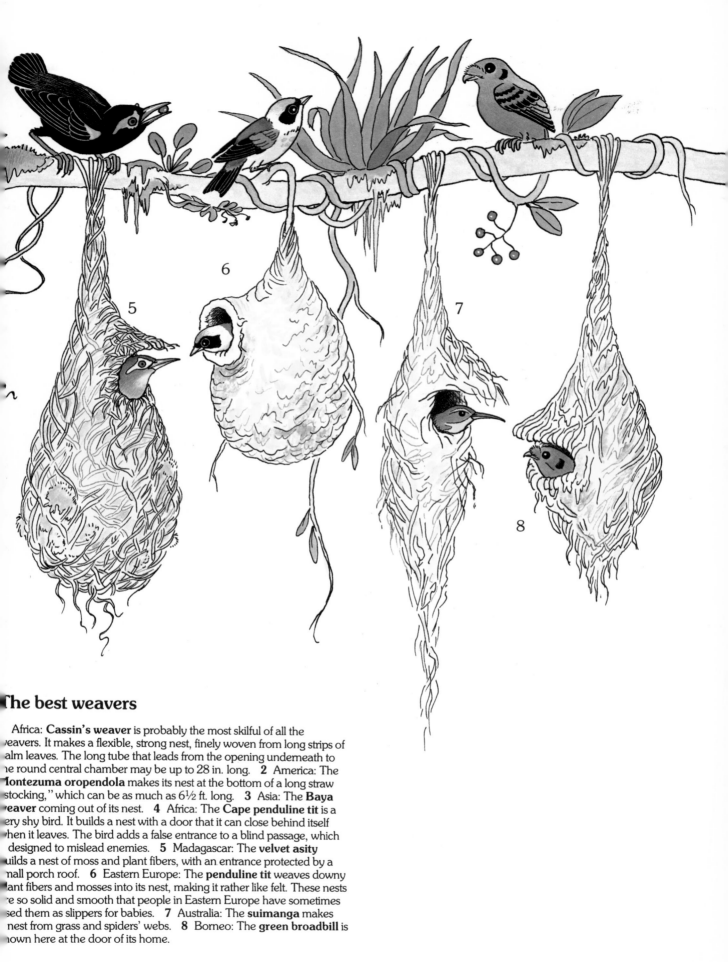

The best weavers

Africa: **Cassin's weaver** is probably the most skilful of all the weavers. It makes a flexible, strong nest, finely woven from long strips of palm leaves. The long tube that leads from the opening underneath to the round central chamber may be up to 28 in. long. **2** America: The **Montezuma oropendola** makes its nest at the bottom of a long straw "stocking," which can be as much as 6½ ft. long. **3** Asia: The **Baya weaver** coming out of its nest. **4** Africa: The **Cape penduline tit** is a very shy bird. It builds a nest with a door that it can close behind itself when it leaves. The bird adds a false entrance to a blind passage, which is designed to mislead enemies. **5** Madagascar: The **velvet asity** builds a nest of moss and plant fibers, with an entrance protected by a small porch roof. **6** Eastern Europe: The **penduline tit** weaves downy plant fibers and mosses into its nest, making it rather like felt. These nests are so solid and smooth that people in Eastern Europe have sometimes used them as slippers for babies. **7** Australia: The **suimanga** makes a nest from grass and spiders' webs. **8** Borneo: The **green broadbill** is shown here at the door of its home.

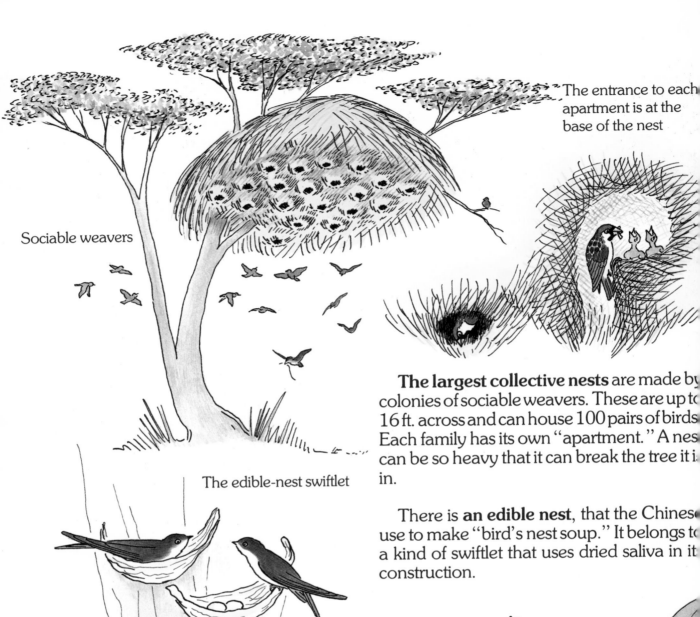

Sociable weavers

The entrance to each apartment is at the base of the nest

The edible-nest swiftlet

The largest collective nests are made by colonies of sociable weavers. These are up to 16 ft. across and can house 100 pairs of birds. Each family has its own "apartment." A nest can be so heavy that it can break the tree it is in.

There is **an edible nest**, that the Chinese use to make "bird's nest soup." It belongs to a kind of swiftlet that uses dried saliva in its construction.

Bee hummingbird

The smallest nests are made by some hummingbirds. This picture shows the bee hummingbird only a little smaller than it is in real life. It is sitting on a delicate nest made of cotton, lichen and spiders' webs.

No nest at all: The fairy tern lays its one egg on a small, bare branch. Once it has hatched, the chick must get used to this lack of comfort.

Fairy tern (chick)

The best mammal architects

The biggest underground towns are made by the prairie dogs of North America. These rodents make large towns, divided into "colonial" burrows. Each small group (or colony) of prairie dogs contains a certain number of families. Members of these families guard their dens fiercely. At the end of the 19th century there were many large prairie-dog towns. One in Texas had about 400 million animals in it. It covered 25,000 sq. mi. – a bigger area than the whole of West Virginia and twice the size of Belgium.

Because farmers waged a merciless war on them, the prairie-dog population has fallen by 90%. The biggest towns today only cover a few dozen acres.

A look out

Prairie dog town

Rattlesnake

A family

The best works of engineering among mammals are made by another kind of rodent – the beavers. These are the only animals that can make dams of branches and mud. They do this to create artificial ponds, which they need for their life in the water.

The biggest beaver dam is on the Jefferson River in the United States. It is 765 yds. long, and it is wide and strong enough for someone to ride across it on horseback.

Beaver city

1 The dam The beaver community has to keep the dam in good condition. The slightest fault is repaired at once. **2 The lookout** If a fox is sighted, the beaver slaps the water with its flat tail to warn the others that danger is approaching. **3 The lodge** A female suckles her young inside the lodge, a rough shelter of sticks and mud, which can only be entered from below water level. **4 The burrow** If the shape

of the bank allows it, the beaver sometimes prefers to dig a burrow into it.
5 **The woodcutter** The beaver has sharp front teeth. It can fell trees up to 8 in. in diameter.

6 **The European red squirrel** and (7) **European harvest mouse** build spherical nests of woven twigs. 8 **The American**

muskrat builds lodges of sticks or digs burrows in the bank like the beaver – but it cannot make dams.

One of the best laid out and most complicated burrows belongs to the American pocket gopher. A spiral tunnel leads to a sleeping chamber, several food storage rooms and a toilet room. The pocket gopher owes its name to the pouches inside its mouth used to carry food. The gopher can move just as quickly backward as forward.

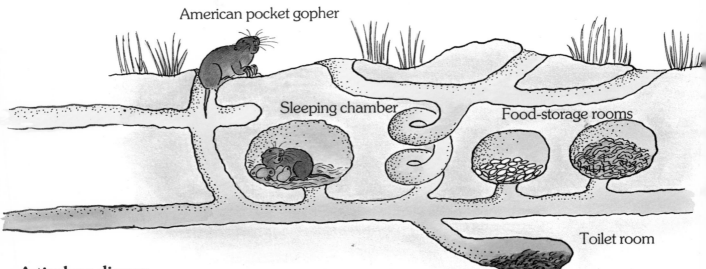

American pocket gopher

Sleeping chamber

Food-storage rooms

Toilet room

A tireless digger

The African aardvark spends the warm hours of the day in its burrow. It is nomadic and makes a new burrow each time it moves. But the old burrows do not stay empty long. Warthogs, ratels, pythons and even leopards shelter in them. The aardvark can dig so fast that it can bury itself instead of running away when it is in danger. The young aardvark spends the first fifteen days of its life in one burrow. After that, it follows its mother as she moves around looking for the termites on which she feeds.

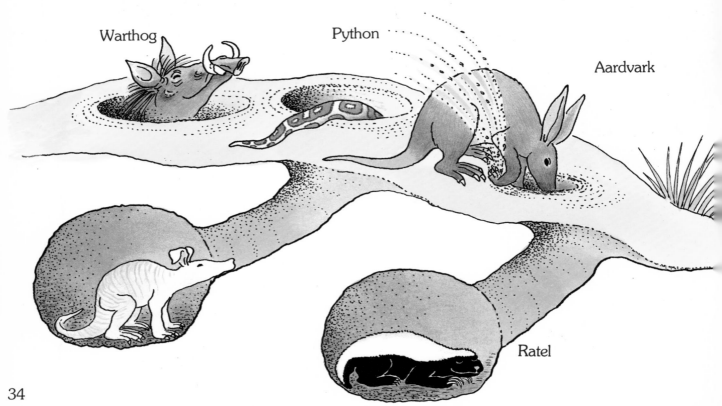

Warthog

Python

Aardvark

Ratel

The best insect architects

The biggest insect structures are those built by termites. There is an African termite (called *Macrotermes bellicosus*) that makes a termitarium from its own excrement mixed with mud. This can be up to 39 ft. high. A scientist named Grassé recorded seeing one that was 328 ft. across, with a village built on it.

Termites also hold the record for depth. They need humid surroundings in order to survive. Termites that live in deserts have to burrow deep into the ground to be near the water that lies there. They may have to go down as far as 130 ft. below the surface.

The workers that achieve all this are blind and only about ½ in. long.

Termite mound

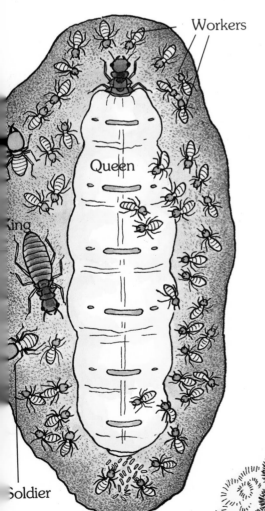

Workers

Queen

King

Soldier

Each termitarium houses a queen, a king, soldiers and a huge number of workers. There can be as many as 10 million termites in one colony.

The queen can be as much as 5½ in. long and over 1 in. wide. She cannot move, and spends her life in her royal cell, being fed by workers. These also gather the 30,000 eggs she lays every day. Since a queen lives for about twenty years, she can be the mother of 21 million termites. Each one lives for only a few months.

Some kinds of termite cultivate fungi inside the nest. They grow it on a cake made with small pieces of bark and rotten wood. They use the fungi to feed the larvae.

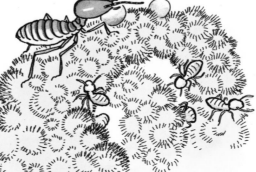

Water

35

Termites and termitaria

SOUTH AMERICA

1 Tree termites **2** Tamandua anteater **3** Giant anteater **4** Six-banded armadillo

AUSTRALIA

5 Constructions made by "**magnetic**" **termites**. These termitaria are always aligned north to south. They are about 16 ft. high. **6** Bruijn's echidna **7** Echidna (spiny anteater)

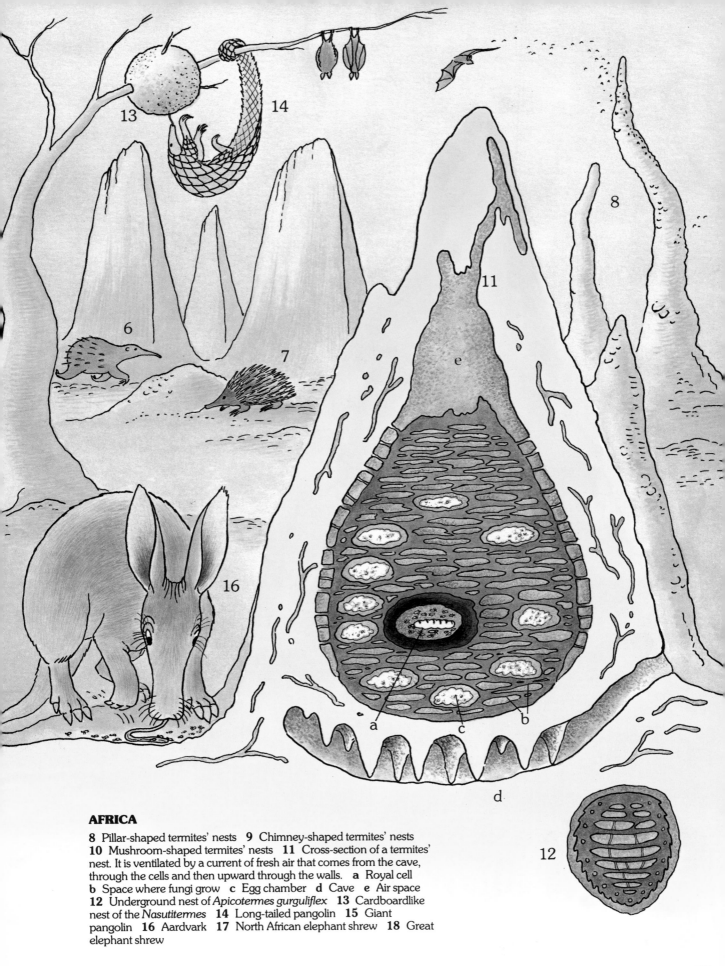

AFRICA

8 Pillar-shaped termites' nests **9** Chimney-shaped termites' nests
10 Mushroom-shaped termites' nests **11** Cross-section of a termites'
nest. It is ventilated by a current of fresh air that comes from the cave,
through the cells and then upward through the walls. **a** Royal cell
b Space where fungi grow **c** Egg chamber **d** Cave **e** Air space
12 Underground nest of *Apicotermes gurguliflex* **13** Cardboardlike
nest of the *Nasutitermes* **14** Long-tailed pangolin **15** Giant
pangolin **16** Aardvark **17** North African elephant shrew **18** Great
elephant shrew

The most impressive ants' nest is made by the little red wood ants.

They build a little hill of twigs, about 6½ ft. high, on top of an old tree stump. The nest also extends downward, into the ground. This area stays warmer in cold weather, so the ants build their winter quarters here.

One of these nests can house a million individuals, including several hundred queens.

Wood-ant nest

"Child labor" is used by Indian weaver ants. These ants build their nests in the leaves of coffee bushes, sewn together with silk threads. While some workers bring the edges of the leaves together, others hold one of their own larvae in their jaws and move it from the edge of one leaf to the edge of another. The larva makes the silken threads needed for the job.

Indian weaver ants

Colobopsis ants, using a "living door"

A "living door" is made by a kind of ant that nests in a tree trunk. A special ant guards the entrance. Its head is flattened and fits the opening exactly. The workers knock at this "door" with their antennae when they want to go inside.

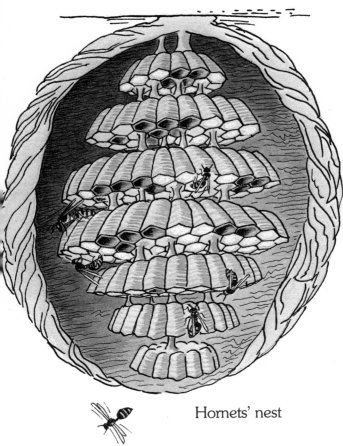

Hornets' nest

Hornets probably invented papier mâché. These social insects are the biggest wasps. They work together, chewing up rotten wood to make a kind of cardboard, which they then use to build their nest.

The nest is made up of a number of layers of hexagonal cells, open at the bottom, which contain the hornet larvae. The entire nest is wrapped in a spherical "envelope," also made of paper.

A hornets' nest can be very large. It may be as much as 6 ft. in diameter.

Amazonian wasps' nest

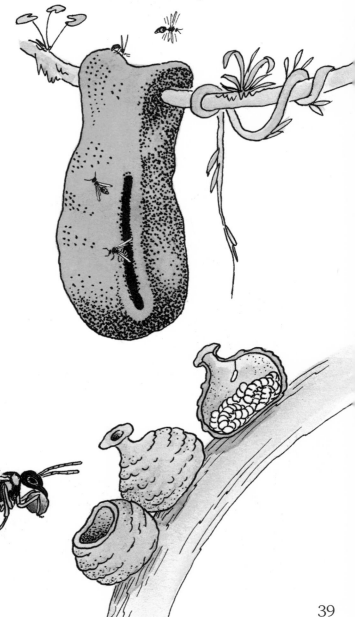

The nest of the Amazonian wasp is made of fine clay and hangs from the branch of a tree. There are several kinds of wasps in this family. The picture shows the nest of one kind. These nests can be 5½ ft. long.

The potter wasp is solitary. It builds small, elegant clay urns and lays a single egg in each one, hanging it from a thread.

The wasp has already placed a pile of grubs at the bottom of each urn. It paralyzes these by stinging them so that when the larva hatches from the egg it has a store of fresh food waiting for it.

Potter wasp with nest

39

Waterworks

Some fish build nests, just as birds do. The picture on the left shows the tunnel-shaped nest of the three-spined stickleback. On the right we can see the nest of the ocellated wrasse. Both are made of weeds.

The nests are shown before the females have laid their eggs. In both cases, the father builds the nest and looks after the young.

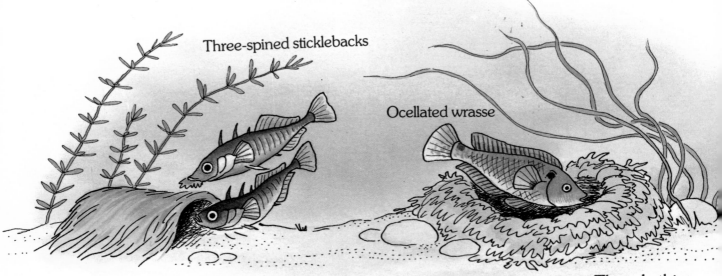

Three-spined sticklebacks

Ocellated wrasse

The Javan flying frog makes "private swimming pools" for its young. When the eggs have been laid, they are surrounded by a slimy liquid. The parents beat this into a froth with their hind legs until it is a mass of foam about 2–3 in. across. They do this on a leafy branch that hangs above the water, so that the foam with the eggs in it sticks to a number of leaves. By the time the eggs hatch, some of this foam has turned to liquid. The tadpoles develop in this liquid until one day a rainstorm washes them off into the water.

Brazilian "blacksmith" tree frogs make a small mud crater about 12 in. across, in shallow water. They lay their eggs here so that the tadpoles can develop safe from hungry fish.

Javan flying frog

Brazilian "blacksmith" tree frog

Rest and play

This section of the book is about the ways that animals amuse themselves when they aren't looking for food or mates.

A sea otter mother and young

The most playful animals

Many animals enjoy playing, even when they are grown-up.

The common otter loves to make slides on muddy riverbanks or, even better, in the snow. It is easy to see that, young or old, they are enjoying themselves.

The sea otter is a very affectionate mother and adores playing with her young. She tosses her baby into the air and then immediately catches it with her paws.

Brown bears have been seen turning somersaults. They roll down grassy slopes and then climb back up, ready to roll down again.

Common otters

Brown bear

Learning through games

Sea lion

Puppy

Mongoose

Gorilla and young

Young animals usually play games that are an important part of learning. Animals play at hunting, fighting, running away, hiding and caring for their young. They do not know how to do many of these things by instinct — they have to learn from other animals of the same kind. This is why animals kept isolated in captivity are often unable to look after themselves when they are released in the wild.

Puppies amuse themselves by trying to catch their own tails.

The young California sea lion plays at throwing stones and fetching them back. It will do this as an adult, using fish.

In captivity, the mongoose invents games for itself. The one shown here has put its head in a cardboard tube and is running around like this.

The young gorilla's mother plays gently with her little one. This develops the bonds of affection between the mother and young.

Lion cubs learn to hunt and to fight by playing with their mother's tail.

Lioness and cubs

Grooming

Bongo (a kind of antelope)

Okapi

Aardwolf

Lowland gorilla

We can tell if an animal is healthy by looking at the condition of its fur or feathers and skin. To keep itself clean, an animal has to be able to reach every part of its body. It is often quite difficult to reach the face and the back.

The okapi uses its very long tongue to clean the whole of its body – including the insides of its ears.

The aardwolf is less gifted – but should not be underestimated. It can curl up its tongue and lick its own muzzle, top and bottom, as far as its eyes.

The antelope can clean its nostrils with its tongue.

For animals lucky enough to have hands or a trunk to help, the solution is obvious. As for animals with long horns, they can scratch their hindquarters without any painful contortions.

Indian elephant

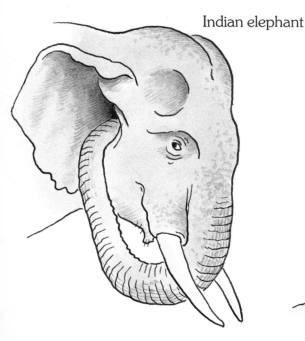

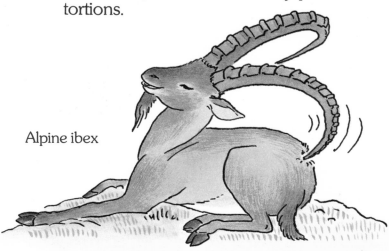

Alpine ibex

Mud baths

Many mammals like to take a mud bath. It can help to soothe the pain of insect stings and dry, itchy skin, and to fight against parasites.

ASIA

1 **Water buffalo** 2 **Indian rhinoceros** 3 **Babirussa**

EUROPE

4 **Wild boar**

AFRICA

5 **Hippopotamus** 6 **Wart hog** 7 **Cape buffalo** 8 **White (or square-lipped) rhinoceros** 9 **African elephant** prefers to wallow in clean water and will travel great distances to find it. To dry itself after a bath, it will use its trunk to sprinkle itself with dust. 10 **Cattle egret** and 11 **Red-billed oxpecker** These two birds are faithful companions to elephants and rhinoceroses. They feed on the insects that torment these great animals. Oxpeckers in particular never leave rhinoceroses, and, as well as getting rid of parasites, they warn their hosts of danger. The rhinoceros has poor sight and needs the birds to alert it.

12 **Domestic pig** and 13 **Human** These two animals can be found just about everywhere! Mud baths are used by many rheumatism sufferers to soothe aches and pains.

5

10

9

11

6

7

8

Pigeons

American blue jay

Crocodile bird

Spur-winged plover

Cleaner shrimp

Vervet monkeys

Scratch my back
Some animals get a friend to help them reach awkward places. Vervet monkeys and pigeons both help each other groom.

Formic acid – a feather conditioner
An ant helps the American blue jay groom – without meaning to! As the bird rubs it over its body, the ant gives out formic acid, which is good for the feathers. Then the bird eats the ant.

Dental care and beauty parlors
The crocodile bird and the spur-winged plover pick out the parasites and scraps of food from crocodiles' jaws. Cleaner shrimps do the same sort of job for fish, cleaning their gills and mouths. They may even try to clean up divers.

The cleaner wrasse runs a "beauty salon" on a coral reef, where fish wait to have parasites removed.

Sea perch being cleaned

Cleaner wrasse

Sleepyheads

The western European hedgehog sleeps eighteen hours a day. It snoozes in its hiding place from six in the morning to six in the evening, sometimes snoring loudly.

During the night, this attractive little mammal takes a couple more naps, each one lasting two to three hours. In between, it goes about looking for food.

All this sleep doesn't alter the fact that it will curl up as soon as the first winter frosts arrive and hibernate until spring.

The two-toed sloth sleeps for fifteen hours a day — but it moves so slowly that it is sometimes hard to tell whether it is asleep or awake.

The big cats sleep for twelve to fourteen hours a day. They spend most of their time resting, on the ground or in trees. They have no natural enemies, so they only need to move when they have to hunt for food. Male lions do not even bother to do that — they leave the work to the females, who either hunt, or steal prey from hyenas.

European hedgehog

Two-toed sloth

Lioness

Lion cub

Gorillas sleep for thirteen hours a day. They wake up late in the morning, and take a two- or three-hour siesta in the hot part of the afternoon.

Troubled sleep

Animals that have to watch out for predators sleep for a very short time, and almost never lie down. The giraffe sleeps deeply for only about twenty minutes a night. This is divided into snatches of five to seven minutes.

Gorilla

Sleeping in the water

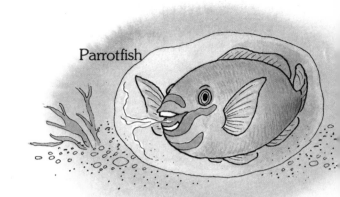

Sea otter

When the sea otter sleeps, it winds seaweed around itself, like a blanket. This stops the otter from drifting away with the currents.

The parrotfish makes a sleeping bag for itself. It has a special gland in its mouth, which it uses to make a kind of bubble. This is probably to protect it from its enemies while it is asleep.

Fish have no eyelids, so they cannot close their eyes. But they do sleep, some lying quite still on the seabed. Some, like this clown triggerfish, lie on one side to sleep.

Some sea mammals float as they sleep, with just their noses out of the water. The California sea lions in the picture hold one flipper out of the water to keep warm. Florida manatees sleep on the bottom and come up every ten or fifteen minutes to breathe. They can do this without waking.

Parrotfish

Clown triggerfish asleep

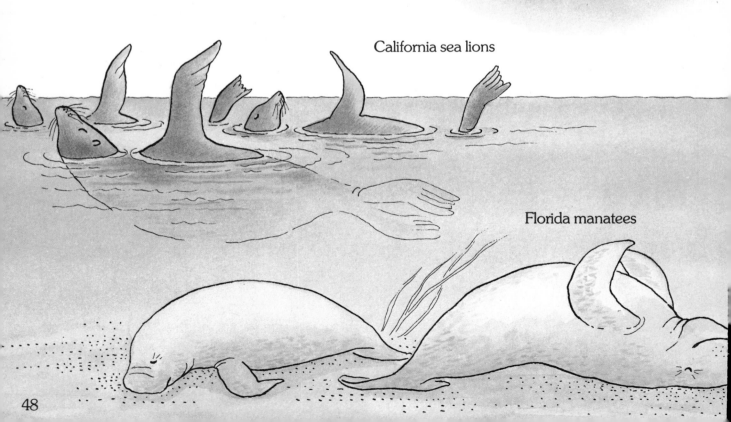

California sea lions

Florida manatees

Winter sleep (hibernation)

In order to survive in cold winter weather, some animals hibernate. This means they fall into a kind of deep sleep. Their body temperature drops and their blood circulation slows down. They remain in hibernation until warmer weather arrives.

Alpine marmot

Northern birch mouse

Bat

Red bat

Whippoorwill

The longest hibernation

The northern birch mouse is a small rodent from northern Europe. It hibernates for eight months of the year, losing half its body weight.

Alpine marmots spend seven to eight months of the year hibernating, curled up inside their winter dens. Their temperature falls to 48°F. and they lose a quarter of their body weight.

Most resistant to cold

Hibernating mammals may wake up occasionally for short periods. Some animals would die if they did not warm up their bodies from time to time. Most wake up every ten to twenty days, but bats can stay unconscious for up to three months. Some, like the red bat, can survive temperatures as low as 23°F. and can even stay alive when partly frozen.

The only bird to hibernate is the American whippoor-will. Others, like the hummingbirds of the Andes, become sluggish for short periods at night.

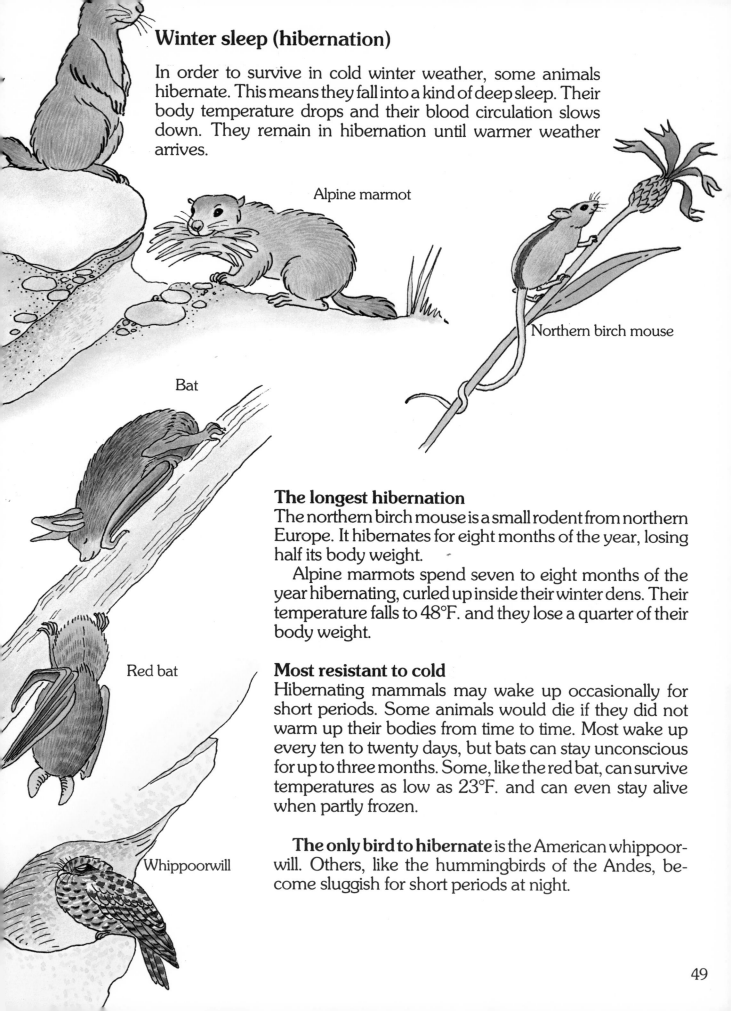

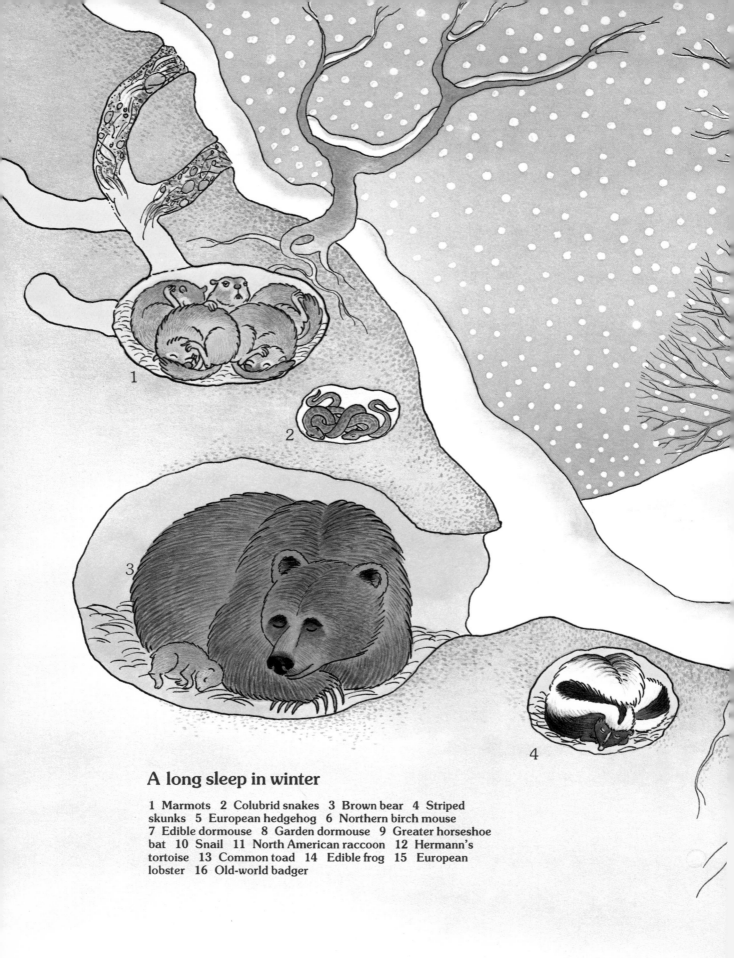

A long sleep in winter

1 Marmots 2 Colubrid snakes 3 Brown bear 4 Striped
skunks 5 European hedgehog 6 Northern birch mouse
7 Edible dormouse 8 Garden dormouse 9 Greater horseshoe
bat 10 Snail 11 North American raccoon 12 Hermann's
tortoise 13 Common toad 14 Edible frog 15 European
lobster 16 Old-world badger

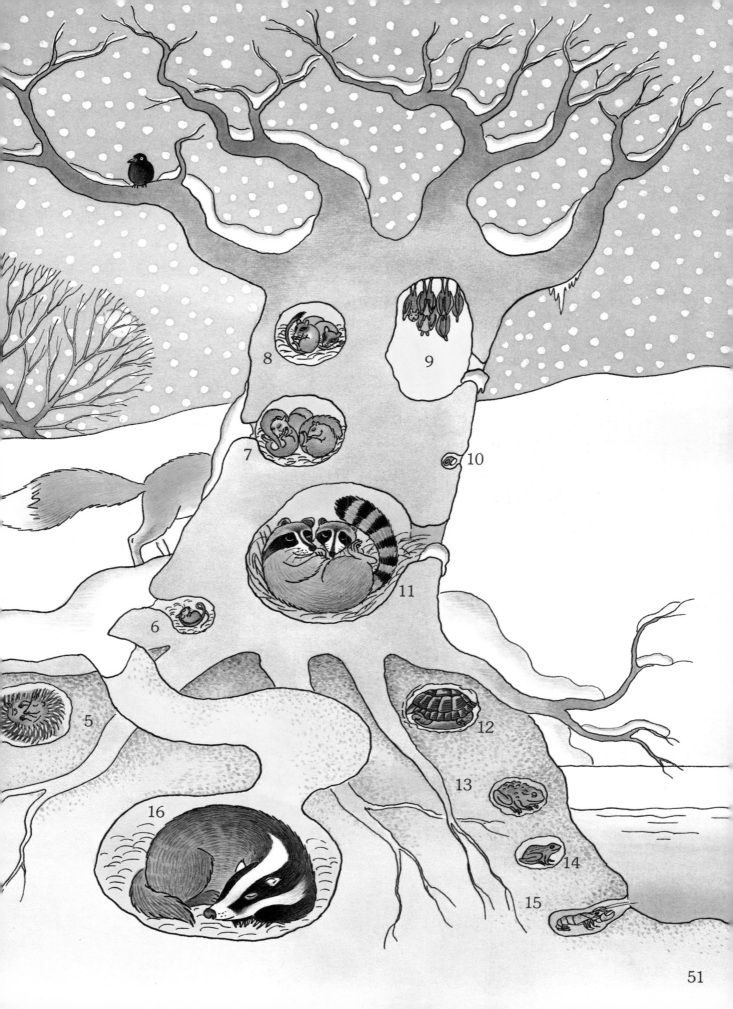

Polar bear and her cubs

An ice palace

The female polar bear hibernates when she is about to have young – the male does not do so at all. In October, she goes into a den made of snow and there, in the depths of winter, one or two cubs are born. They leave the den in February or March.

Summer sleep (aestivation)

Aestivation is similar to hibernation, but it takes place in hot, dry weather. Not many animals aestivate, but one that does is a lungfish that lives in rivers in Africa. In the dry season, it buries itself in mud and is completely inactive. It can stay buried in dry mud for up to four years. As it has lungs as well as gills, it can get oxygen from both air and water. When rain falls and the mud dissolves, the fish becomes active again – unless it has been eaten by a whale-headed stork.

Whale-headed stork

Lungfish

52

Long journeys

Many kinds of animals make long journeys called migrations. They do this to reach a warmer climate where they can spend the winter or to find places where there is more food or to find good breeding grounds.

The Arctic tern has the record for traveling long distances. It nests in the Arctic in the northern summer and flies south to the Antarctic in time for summer there. Later, it returns to the Arctic – a round trip of more than 25,000 mi.

In both the far north and south, it is daylight all the time in summer. For eight months of the year, the Arctic tern never sees the sun set.

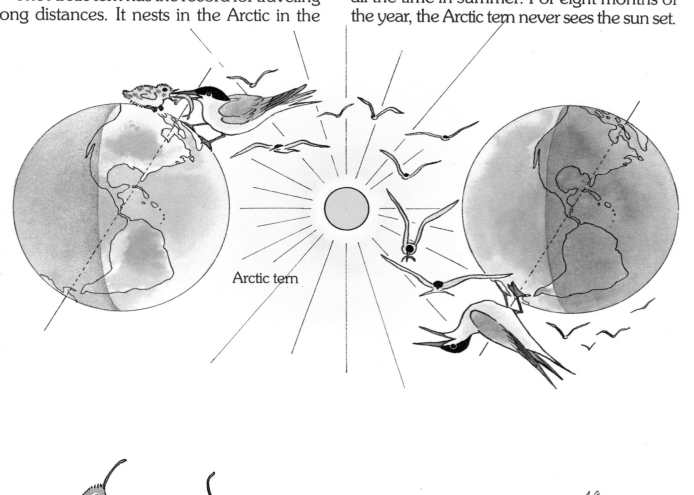

Arctic tern

Mountain quail

The beautiful mountain quail travels on foot. Small groups spend the summer at about 8200 ft. above sea level. Although they can fly, these are really ground-living birds. When bad weather comes, they simply walk single file down to the valleys. When summer returns, they walk back up again in the same way.

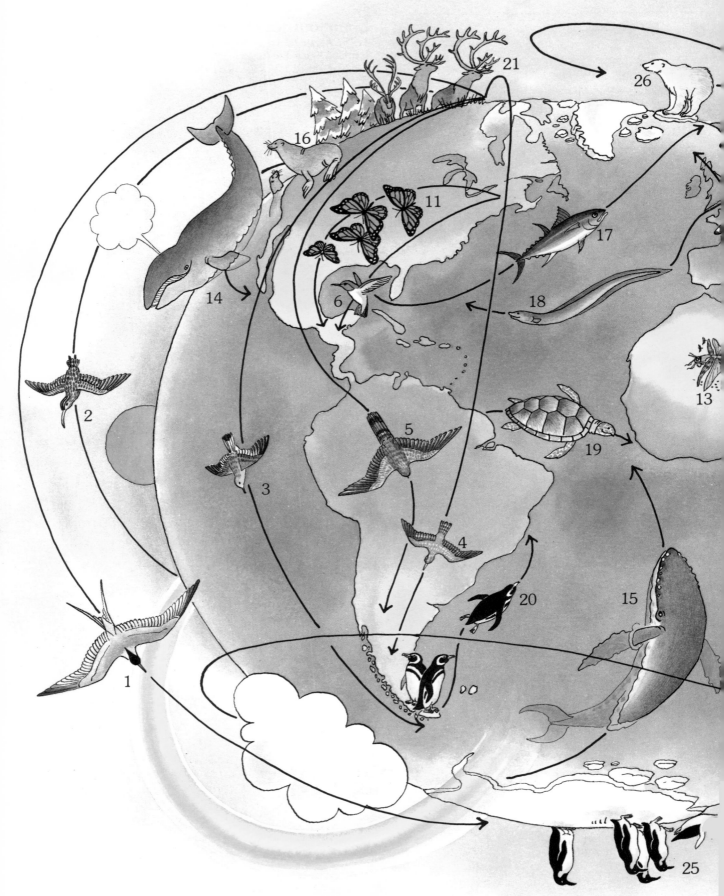

Note: The distances given here are the maximum that each species travels. To make things simpler, the size of the animal is not given.

Long journeys by air

1 The **Arctic tern** spends the northern summer in the Arctic, and the southern one in the Antarctic. This 12,500 mi. journey is an absolute record distance. **2** The **bristle-thighed curlew** spends summer in the Bering Strait and winter in Tahiti, flying a distance of 5500 mi. The curlew holds the record for a nonstop flight over the sea of 2500 mi. **3** The **surfbird** spends the summer in Alaska and flies south to another summer in the Strait of Magellan. It flies 9900 mi. along the west coast of the American continent. **4** The **American golden plover** spends the summer in the Arctic and then flies to Argentina (8000 mi.). This plover is probably the fastest migrant – it can cover 2000 mi. in thirty-five hours, an average speed of 59 mph. **5** The **American peregrine falcon** spends the northern summer in the Bering Strait and the southern one in Argentina. This means flying 8400 mi., a record for a bird of prey. **6** The **ruby-throated hummingbird** spends summer in the Gulf of St. Lawrence and then flies to Nicaragua. This means going 2500 mi. – including 500 mi. nonstop across the Gulf of Mexico. Yet it weighs only ¹⁄₁₀ oz. **7** **European swallows** spend the summer in northern Europe and then fly to South Africa. This is a journey of 6800 mi. **8** The **white stork** spends summer in Europe and then travels 8000 mi. to South Africa. **9** After a summer in Siberia, the **Asian honey buzzard** makes its way 3100 mi. to Indonesia. **10** The **painted lady** holds the record for a butterfly – 2100 mi. from North Africa to Scotland. Some even fly as far as Iceland, a distance of 4000 mi. But they don't survive to return. **11** **Monarch butterflies** migrate in large numbers from the northeastern United States at a rate of 80 mi. a day – for 2100 mi. to Mexico. Here they pass the only winter of their lives. **12** The record holder among bats is the **noctule bat**, which flies 1500 mi. from the Moscow area to Bulgaria. **13** Thousands of millions of **desert locusts** swarm across Africa and the Middle East on a one-way journey, traveling 1000-3000 mi.

By water

14 The **grey whale** spends summer in the Bering Sea and then makes its way to its breeding ground off the coast of Mexico. This 6000 mi. distance is a record distance for a mammal. **15** The **humpback whale** spends the southern summer in the Antarctic and then moves 5000 mi. toward the equator to its breeding ground. **16** The **Alaska fur seal** breeds in summer in the Bering Sea. The females and young migrate south in winter, as far as California, but the males only travel the 3100 mi. to the Gulf of Alaska. **17** One species of **bluefin tuna** swims 4200 mi. across the Atlantic between the Gulf of Mexico and Norway. Another species is born in the Pacific, near the equator, and travels between Japan and Mexico, about 5600 mi. **18** **European eels** travel from European rivers 3700 mi. to the Sargasso sea, where they spawn (lay their eggs). **19** The **green turtle** travels from Surinam to the coast of Ghana – 3700 mi. is the record distance. **20** The **Magellan penguin** is the only bird that migrates by swimming. It travels from its breeding ground in Tierra del Fuego to the sea off Rio de Janiero – 2500 mi.

On foot

21 and **22** **Caribou** and **reindeer** spend the summer in the tundra (grass and lichen) and winter in the Taiga (coniferous forest), traveling 6200 mi. between them. **23** **Saiga antelopes** roam about 200 mi. over the Kalmyk Steppes, looking for food. **24** **Wildebeests** (gnus) travel short distances – about 65 mi. – across the Serengeti plain, in East Africa. **25** **Emperor penguins** travel on floating icebergs 125 mi. from their nesting sites out to sea.

Around the world

26 The ice pack on which **polar bears** live is pulled by sea currents into a slow, circular movement from east to west. This means that, without meaning to, polar bears circle the pole about every five or six years and get back to where they started. **27** Around the world in eighty days: the young northern **sooty albatross** drifts with the wind, circling the world at latitude 40°S. This means that it flies 19,000 mi. in eighty days.

Deadly skyscrapers

At night, the lights of tall buildings and lighthouses attract migrating birds. In the United States, 20,000 birds were killed in one night when they crashed into a skyscraper 1640 ft. high.

Multitudes, past and present

In the 19th century in North America, migrating flocks of more than 2000 million passenger pigeons used to darken the sky for several hours. These birds were killed off by hunters — the last one died in the Cincinnati Zoo in 1914.

By contrast, there are still plenty of desert locusts. These are sometimes called the "scourge of God." In spite of modern methods used to try to control them, thick clouds of up to 10,000 million hungry insects still sometimes fly over North Africa. In 1961, in Morocco, a swarm of these locusts destroyed everything on 1900 sq. mi. of land. They ate 7700 tons of oranges — the amount eaten by people in France in a year.

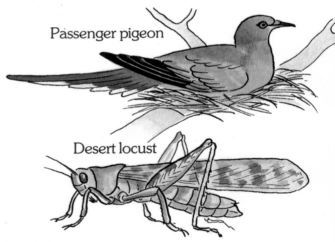

Passenger pigeon

Desert locust

Single file

When American spiny lobsters migrate along the Florida coast, they cling to each other and walk single file on the seabed for more than 60 mi. The long-distance record for crabs and lobsters belongs to the edible crab, which travels 230 mi. along the British coasts.

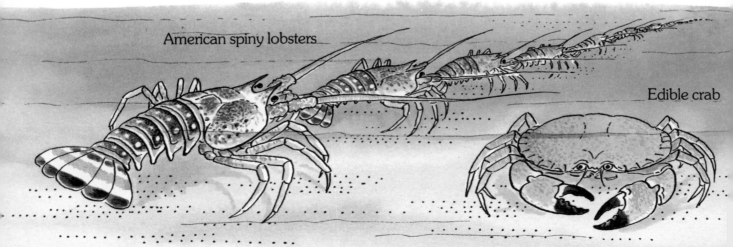

American spiny lobsters

Edible crab

Family life

In this chapter we learn about the ways that animals form pairs and the bonds that parents and young form with each other.

The most attractive males

Male animals have all sorts of ways of trying to attract females. They may dance or sing, present gifts or use scent. The use of colors is especially important.

Female mandrills, for example, are attracted by the male's colored face.

Male birds of paradise are much more brightly colored than the females. They display their colors, using them to attract mates.

The male bowerbird also uses color, but in a different way. First he builds a sort of arch, called a bower. Then he goes out and finds brightly colored objects of all kinds. He lays these out in the bower in order to attract a mate.

Red-plumed bird of paradise

Satin bowerbird

Male mandrill

Dancers

SOLOISTS
1 **Japanese crane** 2 **Crowned crane** 3 **Blue-footed booby**
PAS-DE-DEUX
4 A pair of **western grebes** 5 A pair of **great crested grebes**
6 A pair of **buzzards** 7 Male **turkey vultures** parade in a circle
in front of the females.

Musicians

BELLOWING

8 The **umbrella bird** has a call that sounds like a bull bellowing.
9 **Bullfrogs** are the noisiest amphibians in the world. Their nightly choruses sound like a lowing herd of cattle and can keep everyone awake for several miles around.

PERCUSSION INSTRUMENTS

10 The **three-wattled bellbird** makes a sound like the ringing of a bell or the beating of a drum. **11** The **sage grouse** fills and empties the air sacs on its neck, making a booming sound that can be heard over 300 yd. away. **12** The **greater prairie chicken** makes a thumping sound, rather like a large drum.

CROAKING

13 **Great plain toad** **14** **African sedge frog** **15** **Chorus frog**
16 The **tree frog** has the loudest voice of all the frogs in Europe.
17 The **edible frog** can be heard 550 yd. away. **18** **Lesson's frog**
19 **Natterjack toad** **20** *Physalaemus pustulosis* of South America. It has no common name.

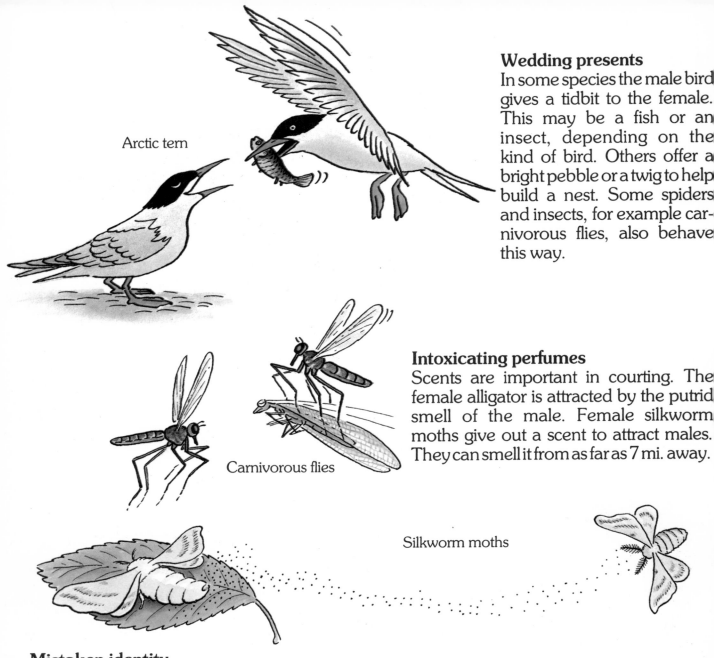

Arctic tern

Wedding presents

In some species the male bird gives a tidbit to the female. This may be a fish or an insect, depending on the kind of bird. Others offer a bright pebble or a twig to help build a nest. Some spiders and insects, for example carnivorous flies, also behave this way.

Carnivorous flies

Intoxicating perfumes

Scents are important in courting. The female alligator is attracted by the putrid smell of the male. Female silkworm moths give out a scent to attract males. They can smell it from as far as 7 mi. away.

Silkworm moths

Mistaken identity

Captive animals sometimes become confused because they are in unnatural surroundings. They may offer affection to the wrong things. A gander once seemed to "fall in love" with a trash can. It refused to pay attention to a more suitable mate.

A male jackdaw once became very fond of a scientist named Konrad Lorenz. It insisted on offering grubs to him, as if he were a female bird—the jackdaw's "fiancée." It tried to put them in his mouth and sometimes even into his ear.

Greylag goose

Jackdaw

The largest harems

A harem is a group of female animals living with one male. Harems form in the mating season. Afterward, the group breaks up and each animal goes its own way.

During the mating season, the males fight quite violently to possess the best territory. From this territory, they try to attract as many females as possible.

The sea elephant and the Alaska fur seal are tied for the record for the biggest harems. There may be up to 150 females.

The mating period for both lasts two months. During this time the males eat nothing. For this reason they are a lot thinner by the end of the mating period, when they go back to life at sea.

Sea elephants

Alaskan fur seals

Many ungulates (animals with hooves) form harems. There may be up to fifty females in a red deer harem. The does (females) take no notice of the male's battles. They may even take advantage of the fact that he is not paying attention and mate with another male while he is busy fighting.

Red deer

Two is company

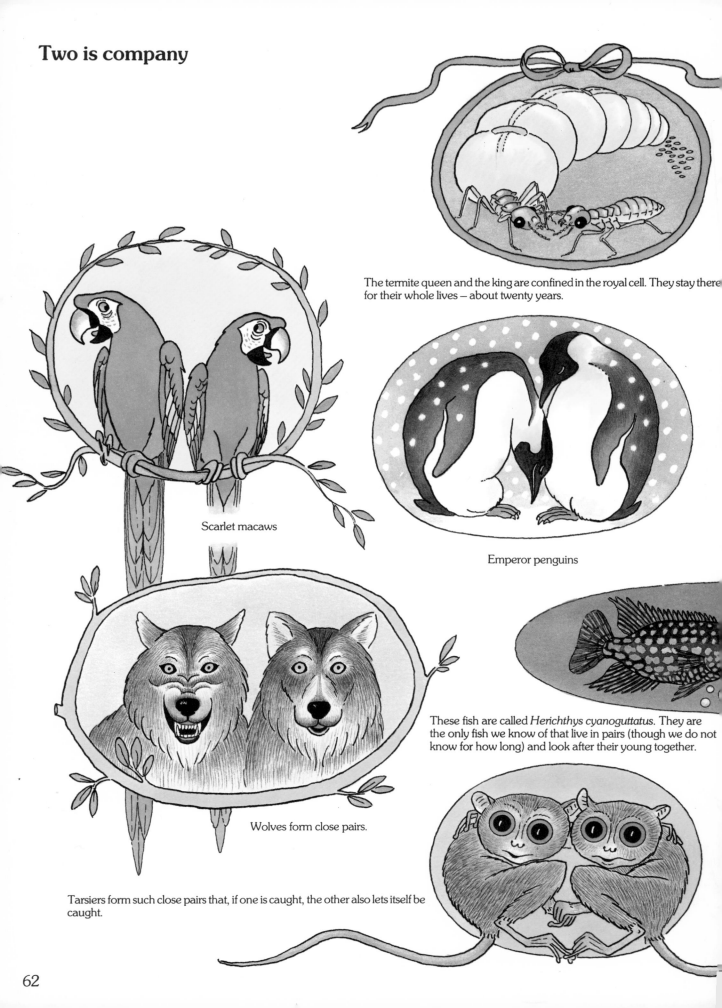

The termite queen and the king are confined in the royal cell. They stay there for their whole lives – about twenty years.

Scarlet macaws

Emperor penguins

Wolves form close pairs.

These fish are called *Herichthys cyanoguttatus*. They are the only fish we know of that live in pairs (though we do not know for how long) and look after their young together.

Tarsiers form such close pairs that, if one is caught, the other also lets itself be caught.

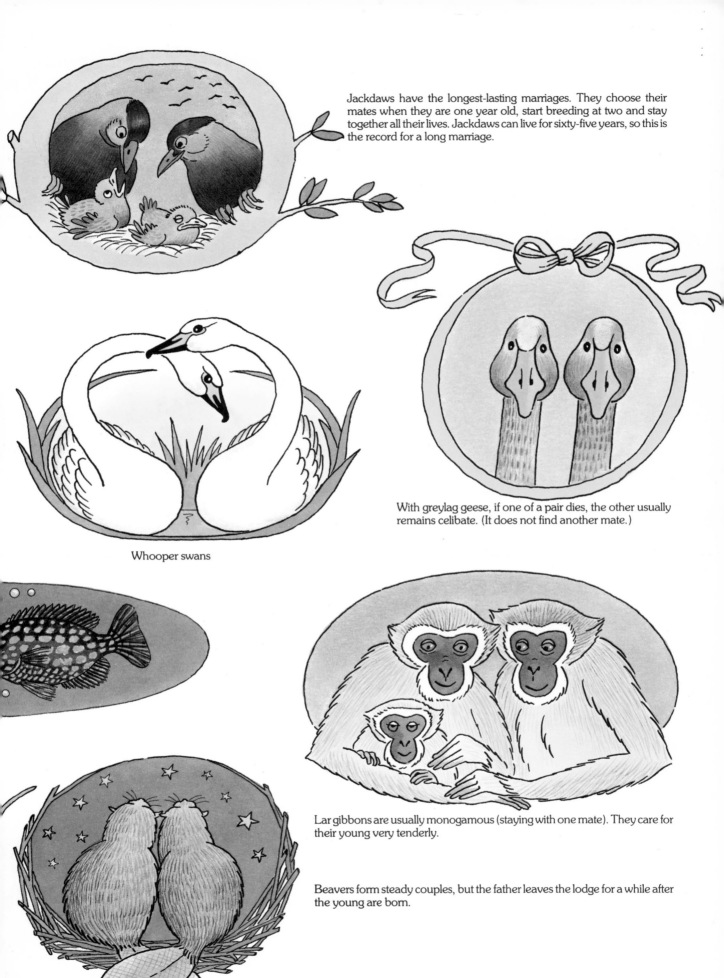

Jackdaws have the longest-lasting marriages. They choose their mates when they are one year old, start breeding at two and stay together all their lives. Jackdaws can live for sixty-five years, so this is the record for a long marriage.

With greylag geese, if one of a pair dies, the other usually remains celibate. (It does not find another mate.)

Whooper swans

Lar gibbons are usually monogamous (staying with one mate). They care for their young very tenderly.

Beavers form steady couples, but the father leaves the lodge for a while after the young are born.

Polyandry

Pheasant-tailed jacana

Polyandry is when one female has several mates. It is very rare. The female jacana visits the nests of different males, one after another. She lays from three to six eggs in each nest. Then she loses interest and the males have to hatch the eggs. A female pheasant-tailed jacana may visit up to ten males.

Naked mole rats

The "queen" of naked mole rats lives underground. These rats live in colonies where only one female, the queen, breeds, rather like queens in some insect colonies. With the help of one or two males, she gives birth to about forty young a year. The other mole rats in the colony have other jobs to do. No other mammals live in this way.

Common toad

Among common toads, many males mate one female. Sometimes there may be as many as twelve at once and the female can suffocate under them all.

Sharks

Sharks have a really strange way of showing their affection. The male swims around after a female, biting her. Fortunately, these wounds heal quickly.

Unusual pregnancies

With most animals the females alone bear the young. But this is not always the case. Here are some examples of male "mothers."

The female seahorse drops her eggs in the male's brood pouch. Twelve days later, he will give birth to the young, which are completely formed by then.

The male *Phyllopteryx taeniolatus* also carries the eggs. He has no brood pouch, so they are stuck to his tail.

The male Darwin's frog swallows the female's eggs. He keeps them in his vocal sac, under his chin, where they develop into tadpoles and then into fully formed frogs. After this, the male gives birth to them through his mouth.

The male midwife toad looks after the female's eggs, keeping them wet until they hatch into tadpoles.

The males of some kinds of *Tilapia* fish keep the eggs in their mouths. The picture shows a *Tilapia* of the *Cichlidae* family.

The female American giant water bug is bigger than the male. She glues her eggs onto the back of her mate, and they stay there until they hatch. He tries to scratch them off, but cannot.

Phyllopteryx taeniolatus

Seahorse

Darwin's frog

Midwife toad

Tilapia

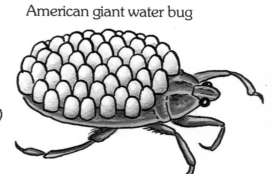

American giant water bug

Emu

The whole job of hatching eggs has to be done by the father emu. He incubates the eggs for two months. During this time, he neither eats nor drinks, and he loses 15 to 18 lbs. When the chicks hatch, he goes on caring for them with the same devotion.

The emperor penguin nests a long way from the sea. After she has laid her egg, the female goes to sea to feed and stock up with fish. The male alone looks after the single egg, keeping it warm on his feet. By the time the female comes back, her cold husband has been several weeks without food. At this time, the chick hatches. The female's stomach is full of fish, so she can feed the chick by regurgitating her food. The male, who is very thin by now, goes off to sea to eat. By this time many males are so weak that they never make it.

Emperor penguin

Incredible pregnancies in frogs and toads

The female of the little Australian frog called *Rheobatrachus silus* keeps her eggs in her stomach. They stay there until the young are fully developed. The eggs contain a substance that stops the frog's gastric juices from harming them – otherwise they would be digested along with the frog's food. The young frogs come up out of the stomach and leave through their mother's mouth.

The incredible Surinam toad and the frog called *Fritziana goeldii* both have dorsal pregnancies. The eggs hatch from pouches on the females' backs.

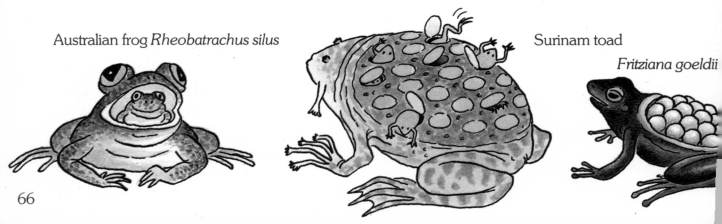

Australian frog *Rheobatrachus silus*

Surinam toad

Fritziana goeldii

Gorillas

Heroic parents

Some animals lay millions of eggs to make sure their species survives. Many eggs will be destroyed – but there will always be some left. Other kinds of animals produce only a few eggs or just one, and so they take great care to protect their young. They may even be ready to die for them.

Gorillas protect their young very bravely. To capture one young gorilla, a poacher has to kill all the adults in the family.

The little ringed plover pretends to be wounded to attract the attention of a predator. Then it draws the enemy away from the nestlings.

Anyone who goes near the Nile crocodile's eggs runs a great risk. The parents stay near the nest and are not afraid to attack. Once they have hatched, the young are gently carried to the river. The parents go on watching over them for another month or two.

Most of the animals that care for their young are mammals or birds. Invertebrates (animals without backbones) usually do not provide so much care. But some do. This octopus is standing guard over its eggs.

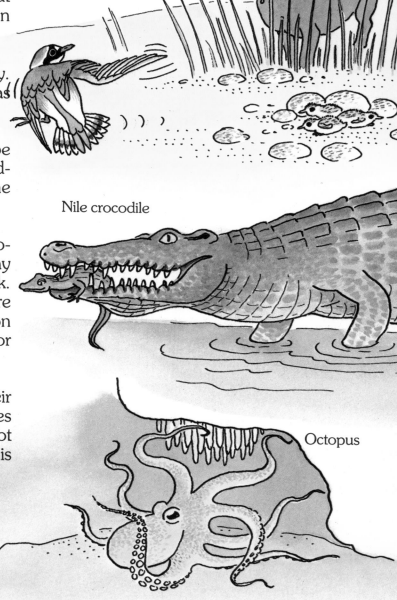
Ringed plover

Nile crocodile

Octopus

Living fortresses — group defense

1 A herd of **African elephants** is made up of females and young. The mothers use their bodies to protect the young. **2** Male **baboons** attack a leopard while the females run away with the young. **3** **Musk oxen** stand in a circle around their young and will not run away, whatever happens. This offers protection from wolves, but it means a human can shoot the whole herd without a single animal moving. **4** A shark that comes near a wounded or sick **dolphin** will be attacked by the other dolphins. They stab it to death with their beaked snouts. **5** A group of **lapwings** will mob (attack) a crow and can drive it away. They confuse it by calling and spinning around it in the air. **6** A group of **jackdaws** may attack anyone holding anything dark. They think it is a jackdaw in danger.

Help for the wounded

Lioness and cubs

Lionesses bring up several litters of cubs together. We know of one lioness who found food for her wounded sister as well as looking after the eight cubs they had between them.

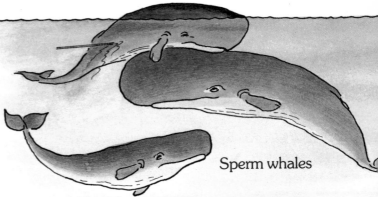

Coyotes

Male and female coyotes form close pairs that look after each other. A female was once seen bringing food to her mate, who had injured his leg.

Marine mammals are famous for the way in which they help a sick or wounded relative. They keep it on the water's surface for as long as possible to prevent it from drowning. The picture shows sperm whales.

Sperm whales

When African hunting dogs go out to find food, mothers and young puppies are left behind. The hunters kill food for the whole pack. They regurgitate some of the food they have eaten to feed the young pups and their mothers. If a mother dies, the orphans are adopted at once. The pack also feeds sick and wounded males.

African hunting dogs

Mourning

When a lion kills a zebra, the rest of the herd take no notice. But elephants show obvious grief when a relative dies. They try to support a dying elephant and put it back on its feet. When it no longer shows any sign of life, they watch over the body for days before they leave it — having first covered it with leaves and earth. A female elephant was once seen carrying her dead calf on her tusks, refusing to be separated from it.

Elephant and calf

The bond between a mother chimpanzee and her young is very strong. The scientist Jane Goodall has written about a young chimpanzee called Flint, aged eight. After his mother died, he was so upset that, three weeks later, he also died on the very same spot.

Chimpanzees

The 18th century naturalist, Stellar, described how sea cows rescued wounded relatives and tried to pull the spears out of their sides. He once saw a male come back for several days to the place where his dead partner lay — as if he could not stay away. Stellar was the only naturalist to report about these animals, because they were all killed off soon after his study.

Sea cows

Acts of violence

Chimpanzees

We like to read about animals behaving in ways we admire – but we are not so happy about them when they behave badly!

Monkey warfare
Each group of chimpanzees lives in a territory where there are no other chimpanzees. The males patrol the boundaries of their territories. If they meet any "foreigners" there can be violent quarrels and even murder.

Infanticide
Infanticide (killing the young) is common among lions and tigers. When a new dominant male takes over a group, he often kills the young of the old dominant male and then eats them.

There is a story of a female chimpanzee who went mad. She killed and ate the newly born young in her group, sharing them with her own young.

Fratricide means killing among brothers and sisters. Young sand sharks do this – even before they are born.

Tigers

Sand shark young inside their mother

Communication

Now we will find out about the ways animals communicate among themselves – and how people try to communicate with animals.

Animals talk to each other

Humans are certainly the most talkative of all animals, with a spoken vocabulary of at least 40,000 words. But we are not the only talking creatures. There are other animals that have a simple kind of language of their own. This makes it possible for them to call their young, warn others of danger, express their own moods and so on.

The language of crows is the most complicated. Researchers have listed many different sounds or "words" made by crows. There are about 300 of these. But, unfortunately, no one knows what most of them mean. So we still cannot understand what crows are talking about when they gather together in the fields.

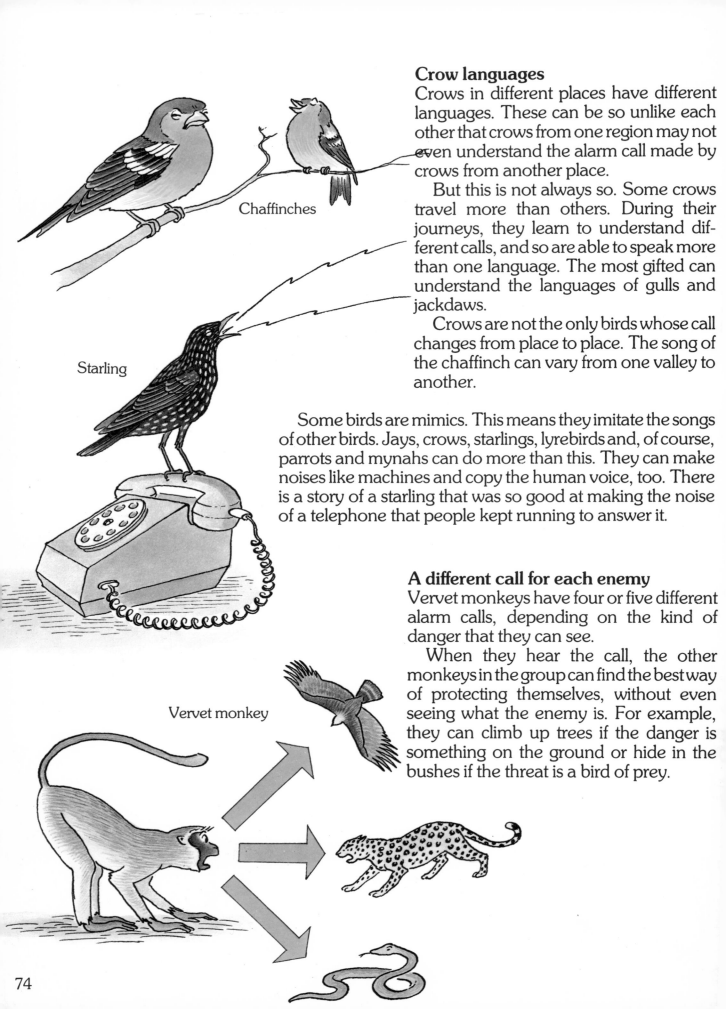

Crow languages

Crows in different places have different languages. These can be so unlike each other that crows from one region may not even understand the alarm call made by crows from another place.

But this is not always so. Some crows travel more than others. During their journeys, they learn to understand different calls, and so are able to speak more than one language. The most gifted can understand the languages of gulls and jackdaws.

Crows are not the only birds whose call changes from place to place. The song of the chaffinch can vary from one valley to another.

Some birds are mimics. This means they imitate the songs of other birds. Jays, crows, starlings, lyrebirds and, of course, parrots and mynahs can do more than this. They can make noises like machines and copy the human voice, too. There is a story of a starling that was so good at making the noise of a telephone that people kept running to answer it.

A different call for each enemy

Vervet monkeys have four or five different alarm calls, depending on the kind of danger that they can see.

When they hear the call, the other monkeys in the group can find the best way of protecting themselves, without even seeing what the enemy is. For example, they can climb up trees if the danger is something on the ground or hide in the bushes if the threat is a bird of prey.

Chaffinches

Starling

Vervet monkey

The loudest voices

Rorqual

Sperm whale

Humpback whale

Animals often have to call loudly so that they can be heard as far away as possible. These loud calls may be made to attract a mate, to claim territory or to give the alarm.

The common rorqual whale sings at a frequency of 20 hertz (twenty sound wave vibrations per second). It can be heard 100 mi. away. We think that in the past, before there were so many ships to interfere with the sound, the rorqual could be heard for more than 600 mi.

The humpback whale makes a call that sounds musical even to humans. The sperm whale communicates by making a drumming noise like a galloping horse.

Siamang

The siamang (a gibbon) is the noisiest of all land animals. It has an air sac that it inflates when it calls. This makes it possible to hear the call 5 mi. away.

When two troops of howler monkeys meet, the males scream at each other. After this, the two groups part without ever actually fighting.

Howler monkeys

Body language

Talking is only one way of communicating. Dance, singing and facial expression are other ways — for people as well as for other animals.

EXPRESSIONS

▼ An expressive face has to have mobile facial muscles. These are found only in primates (apes, humans and monkeys — especially chimpanzees). Whatever it looks like to you, this mandrill's expression is friendly! The horse is not laughing, but yawning.

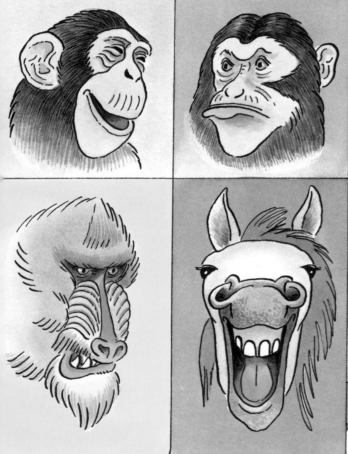

Chimpanzee

Mandrill   Horse

EARS

▶ Usually, when an animal pricks up its ears it is being friendly. But when it lays them back it is a sign of aggression or fear.

The expressions of the cats and zebras in the left-hand pictures are friendly, but those on the right are not!

There are exceptions to this rule — when an elephant's ears stand up, it is best avoided!

DANCE

▲ The honeybee dances when it returns to the hive. This dance carries a message about the direction and distance the other bees must go to find food. It also tells them what kind of food it is, and how much. The dancer makes a figure 8. The angle of this figure shows the angle between the food and the sun. The nearer the food, the faster the dance.

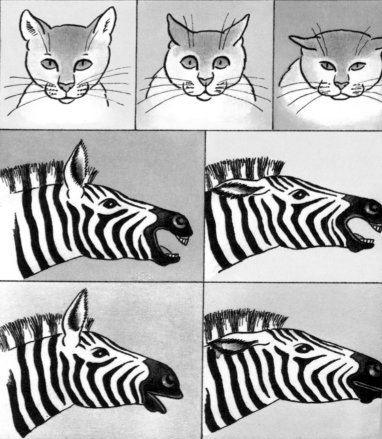

TEETH
◄ None of these smiles is friendly. By showing its teeth, each of these animals is saying "I am dangerous and I will attack you if you don't go away."
▼ Displays of claws, horns and talons carry the same message.

HOOVES
◄ The bull scratches the ground with its front hoof. This shows it is angry and ready to charge.

HANDS
◄ In primates, especially humans, hands are used to express things. Here, a chimpanzee is asking for food.

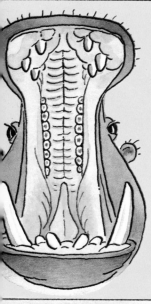

FEATHERS AND FUR
Fluffing up feathers or fur can make an animal look bigger and more impressive to an enemy. This is both aggressive and defensive. ▼

The pronghorn antelope fluffs up a tuft of white hair on its rump to show danger is near. ▼

TAILS
► Dogs use their tails to show their feelings. The top picture shows friendly trust. Next comes threat, then uncertainty, friendly submission and, at the bottom, complete submission.

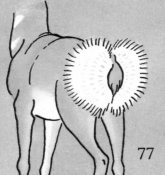

Tragic misunderstandings

Different kinds of animals express themselves in different ways – so they can easily misunderstand each other.

Kangaroo versus deer

A red kangaroo was once put in the same enclosure as an American stag. Everything was all right as long as the kangaroo stayed crouching in a corner. But as soon as it began jumping around, the deer attacked it with its hooves. This was because the kangaroo was standing up on its back legs. This is normal for a kangaroo, but to the deer this was a clear sign of aggression, and it wanted to fight back.

Turkey versus peacock

When two turkeys fight, the one that is losing lies down on the ground. The winner stops attacking it at once and just struts around making threatening signs. In a fight between a turkey and a peacock, the peacock nearly always comes off best. The peacock attacks by leaping into the air and striking its opponent with the powerful claws on its feet. The turkey is frightened by this and quickly lies down in front of the attacker. But the peacock does not understand. It goes on attacking the turkey and will kill it unless someone puts a stop to the fight.

e language of smells

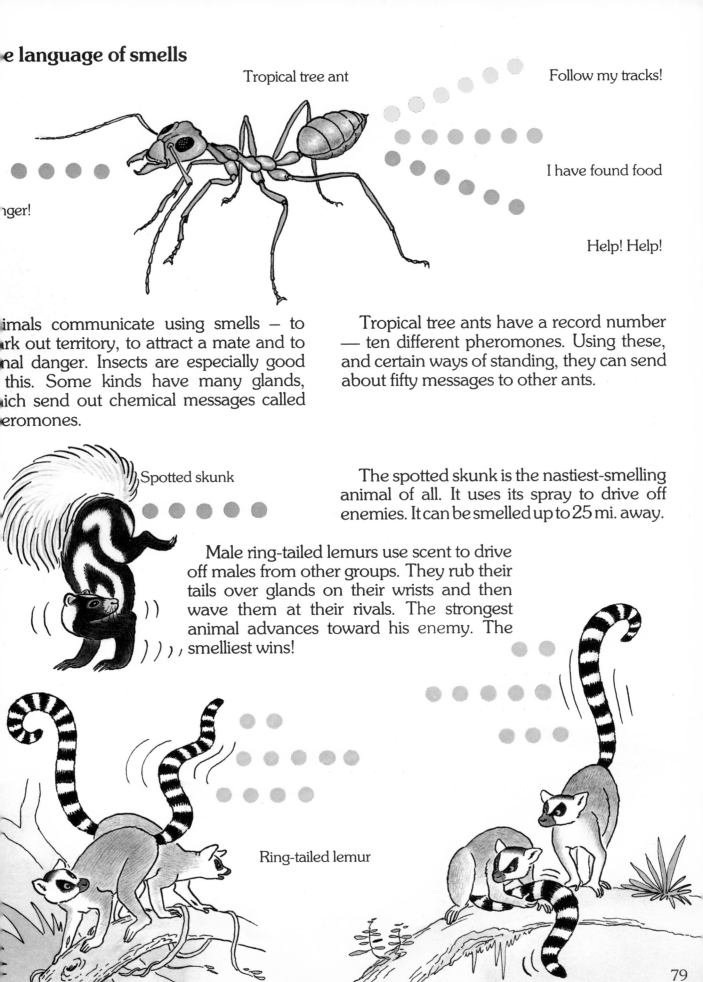

Tropical tree ant

Follow my tracks!

I have found food

Help! Help!

nger!

imals communicate using smells — to rk out territory, to attract a mate and to nal danger. Insects are especially good this. Some kinds have many glands, ich send out chemical messages called eromones.

Tropical tree ants have a record number — ten different pheromones. Using these, and certain ways of standing, they can send about fifty messages to other ants.

Spotted skunk

The spotted skunk is the nastiest-smelling animal of all. It uses its spray to drive off enemies. It can be smelled up to 25 mi. away.

Male ring-tailed lemurs use scent to drive off males from other groups. They rub their tails over glands on their wrists and then wave them at their rivals. The strongest animal advances toward his enemy. The smelliest wins!

Ring-tailed lemur

Conversations with people

People have always had the dream of being able to talk to animals. There are many stories and legends about this happening. Even today, people are fascinated by the idea, and there is always argument about it in the scientific world.

The story of "Clever Hans"

Modern scientists who try to communicate with animals have to be very careful. They cannot forget the story of Professor Van Osten and his horse, called "Clever Hans."

In 1904, the professor, who was a famous mathematician, said that his horse could read, write and add. He really believed it. Professor Van Osten would ask Hans a question, and the horse would answer by tapping his hoof on the ground the correct number of times.

Of course, a great many people were interested in this story. Unluckily for Van Osten, another scientist made a study of what was really happening. He discovered that the horse was watching his master's fa and "reading" the replies there.

Hans could see tiny changes in the profe sor's expression — so slight that no one e had noticed them. From these he could wo out exactly when it was time to stop stam ing. If the person asking the questions w hidden by a screen, or did not know t answer himself, then the horse could not the trick and answer the questions.

Professor Van Osten was very d appointed. But it is still amazing that Ha was clever enough to notice the slight changes in the expressions on his maste face and know what they meant.

...hoe makes a sign for "dirty monkey" ...e watches this little macaque. She ...s of herself as a human being.

It is not surprising that the first animals people have tried communicating with are our closest relatives. The first experiments were disappointing. Vicki, a female chimpanzee who had been brought up with a human family, managed to say four English words, but she found it very difficult. Then, in 1966, her "family" had a brilliant idea. They taught her chimpanzee sign language. From then on, progress was amazing.

...hoe's first word:
...re!"
...nples of phrases:
...e me sweet."
...me hug me again."
...y."

A young chimpanzee named Washoe has a vocabulary of 130 sign words. She has been learning for five years and can make phrases of five or six words.

Washoe can explain what she wants and how she feels. She can insult her companions and show that she has a sense of humor. One odd thing is that Washoe seems to think she is a person — not a chimpanzee.

The experiment is still going on. Some chimpanzees actually communicate with each other using this sign language and are teaching it to their young. Who knows where it will all end?

...here is a thirteen-year-old gorilla named ...o who has 1000 sign words in her ...abulary. She uses 500 of these regularly. ... has been studying with her teacher, ...ny Patterson, for thirteen years.
...oko seems to understand everything that ...aid to her and communicates very well ... people. She has even shown that she ... tell lies now and then!
...he is very fond of her cat, which she ...cribes in signs as: "Soft good cat cat."
...nlike Washoe, Koko does not think of ...self as a human being, and she likes to ...cribe herself as what she is. She seems ...y proud of being a gorilla, for she calls ...self: "Fine animal gorilla."

Koko makes the sign for "bad" after she has been naughty.

First contacts

Perhaps we will find a lost paradise, through learning to communicate with the animals.

1 **Arli**, an English setter, types a few words on a specially designed typewriter.   2 **Lucy** has a sign conversation in American sign language, with Roger Fouts (Institute of Primate Studies, USA).   3 **Sarah** communicates using magnetized chips with abstract shapes (in a study by David Premack, USA).   4 **Lana** communicates by pressing keys that have symbols drawn on them (Yerkes regional Primate Research Center, USA).   5 **Koko** learns to use an electronic brain linked to a word synthesizer.   6 **Koko** knows very well how to use a camera.
7 In Indonesia, Professor Galdikas takes care of young **orangutans** which have been captured illegally by traders.

She has a "rehabilitation camp," where she prepares them for a return to life in the wild. While at the camp, they learn the basics of sign language. **8** When they get the chance, young **chimpanzees** are enthusiastic abstract painters. (Studied by the zoologist Desmond Morris, in England.) **9** Rather than teach animals a human language, Professor Konrad Lorenz preferred to talk to them in their own. This is what he used to say to his geese: "Ga-gi-ga ga-ga-ga." **10** No one has made much of a study of the intellectual possibilities of **elephants**. But there are reports of an Indian elephant that writes a few words on a blackboard. An elephant from the Syracuse Zoo (USA) recently produced some interesting drawings.

Talking with a bird

African parrots have a great talent for in[i]tating human voices. People have know[n] about this for a very long time. A cardinal [in] the 19th century once spent a fortune tr[y]ing to get a parrot that could recite the ent[ire] Nicene Creed.

There are also parrots that can spe[ak] several languages and others that can p[er]form in comedy shows with several parro[ts] taking part. The best speaking parrots ha[ve] learned about 300 words.

African grey parrot

We used to think that birds do not understand what they are saying. But the scientist Irene Pepperberg proved that her grey parrot, Alex, could identify more than fifty objects and could ask for them and refuse them in English.

Talking with a dolphin

Scientists are very interested in dolphins' intelligence, but it is not easy to make contact with them because they live in water. A scientist named Dr. John C. Lilly claimed dolphins could imitate human voices – but recordings do not show this. People have tried using gestures, plastic tokens and whistling, but conversations until now have all been one-way. The dolphins understand messages, such as: "Fetch the ball!" – but who knows what they might want to say to us?

We think that possibly the most intelligent animals of all are the great whales – but the problem is how to study them. We can't keep them in aquariums!

Alex refuses a cup of coffee

Talking to dolphins

The most intelligent animals

Using the sign language of the deaf, Koko the gorilla took the same sorts of intelligence tests that children take. At the age of seven, she had an IQ (intelligence quotient) of between 85 and 95. But we do not know if that means that gorillas are the most intelligent animals. There is no way of comparing Koko's intelligence with that of an animal that has no words — an elephant, for example.

Sense of humor

Some people think that only people have a sense of humor — but this is not so. Washoe the chimpanzee had a rather nasty sense of humor. Once, when she was sitting on her teacher's shoulders, she urinated on him and then said that this was "funny."

Koko

Recognizing themselves and others

Gorillas and chimpanzees can recognize themselves in photographs and in a mirror. Social animals such as crows, elephants and wolves know members of their own group as individuals and can often pick out the humans they know.

These abilities are not only found in birds and mammals. There was once an octopus that could recognize the woman who fed it. When it heard her footsteps, it would get restless and change color. If someone else appeared, it showed signs of disappointment.

Washoe, showing she has a sense of humor

A gorilla looks at itself in a mirror

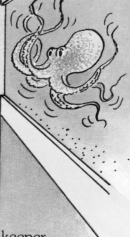

An octopus recognizes its keeper

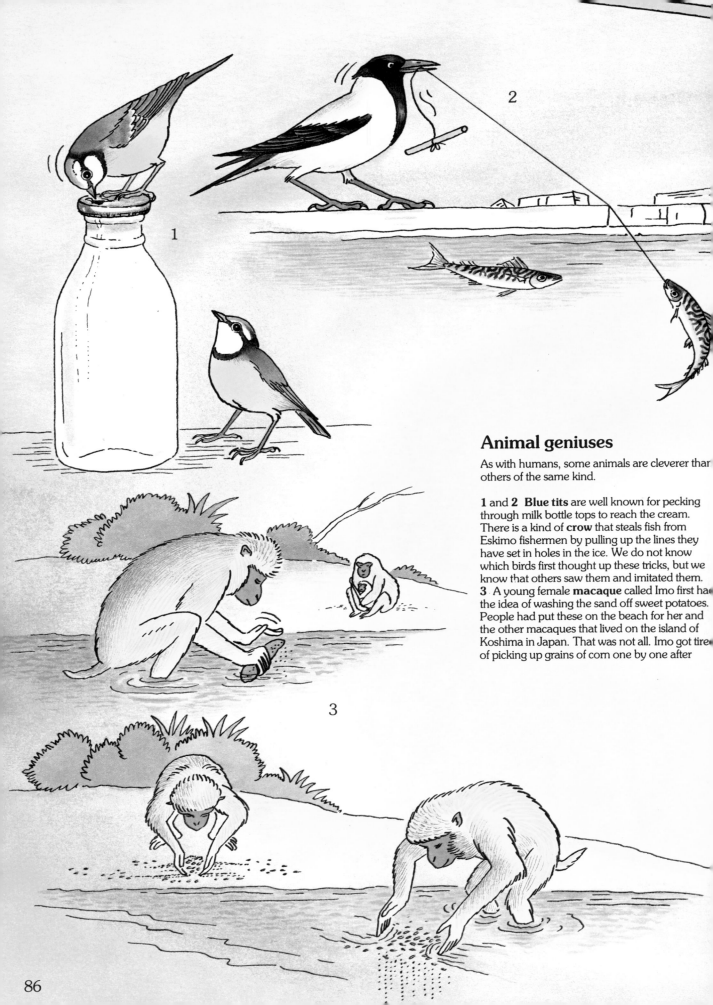

Animal geniuses

As with humans, some animals are cleverer than others of the same kind.

1 and **2 Blue tits** are well known for pecking through milk bottle tops to reach the cream. There is a kind of **crow** that steals fish from Eskimo fishermen by pulling up the lines they have set in holes in the ice. We do not know which birds first thought up these tricks, but we know that others saw them and imitated them.
3 A young female **macaque** called Imo first had the idea of washing the sand off sweet potatoes. People had put these on the beach for her and the other macaques that lived on the island of Koshima in Japan. That was not all. Imo got tired of picking up grains of corn one by one after

5

cientists had spread them on the sand. She
howed again how clever she was. She took a
handful of corn mixed with sand and sprinkled it
on the surface of the water. The sand sank, but
he corn floated, and she could collect it easily.
The other monkeys soon learned to copy both
ricks.   **4** A **chimpanzee** in captivity wanted a
bunch of bananas that had been tied too high for
t to reach. It solved the problem by piling up
boxes and climbing up the pile.   **5** An **orang-
utan** named Katjong, in a zoo at Nuremberg in
Germany, learned to make hammocks and
swings for itself by knotting cloths together.

4

Jobs for the monkeys

Macaques collecting coconuts

Baboon shepherd

Baboon shepherd
A female chacma baboon in South Africa turned out to be a very good shepherd. She watched carefully over a flock of goats, taking them to their pasture each morning and bringing them back in the evening. She also carried newborn kids under her arm when they were too weak to walk, and even helped them to suck from their mothers.

Coconut pickers
Pig-tailed macaques in Sumatra have the job of collecting coconuts from coconut palms. It is easier for them to climb the trees than it is for people.

Monkey nurses
There is a kind of monkey in Gabon that is very good at removing chigoe fleas from people's feet. It is much better at this than people are themselves. The female of these fleas burrows through the outer layer of skin. Then her abdomen, which is full of eggs, swells up. This causes itching. Getting the flea out is difficult because it is important not to tear the container of eggs and leave them in the skin.

Monkey removing fleas

INDEX

Sloth, 47
Snail, 51
Snake, 21
  Colubrid, 50
  coral, 21
  egg-eating, 9, 10
  Okinawa habu, 10
  scarlet king, 21
Song thrush, 19
Sooty albatross, 55
Sperm whale, 70, 75
Spider
  garden, 14
  line weaver, 15
  Myrmecium, 16
  Nephila, 13
  purse-web, 14
  Retiarius, 14
  Stegodyphus, 13
  stick, 13
  water, 15
  web-casting, 14
Spider crab, 22
Spiny anteater, 36
Spiny lobster, 56
Sponge crab, 23
Spotted skunk, 79
Spotted triggerfish, 48
Spur-winged plover, 46
Square-lipped rhinoceros, 45
Squid, 24
Squirrel, 12
  red, 33

Starling, 74
Stegodyphus, 13
Stellar (naturalist), 71
Stick spider, 13
Stickleback, three-spined, 40
Stork
  whale-headed, 52
  white, 54
Striped shrimpfish, 22
Striped skunk, 50
Suimanga, 29
Surfbird, 54
Surinam toad, 66
Swallow, 55
Swan, whooper, 63
Swiftlet, 30

T

Tailorbird, 27
Tamandua anteater, 36
Tarsier, 62
Termite, 17, 20, 34-37, 62
Tern
  Arctic, 53, 54, 60
  fairy, 30
Three-spined stickleback, 40
Three-wattled bellbird, 59
Thrush, 19
Tiger, 11, 72
Tilapia, 65

Tit
  blue, 86
  penduline, 28, 29
Toad
  common, 51, 64
  great plain, 59
  midwife, 65
  natterjack, 59
  Surinam, 66
Tortoise, 19
  Hermann's, 51
Tree ant, 79
Tree frog, 59
  "blacksmith," 40
Triggerfish, 48
Tuna, bluefin, 54
Turkey, 78
Turkey vulture, 59
Turtle, green, 54
Two-toed sloth, 47

U

Umbrellabird, 59

V

Van Osten, Professor, 80
Velvet asity, 29
Vervet monkey, 46, 74
Vulture
  Egyptian, 19
  turkey, 59

W

Warthog, 34, 45
Wasp, 39
Water buffalo, 44
Water bug, 65
Water scorpion, 15
Water spider, 15
Weaver ant, 38
Weaverbird, 27
Web-casting spider, 15
Whale, 84
  blue, 9
  grey, 54
  humpback, 13, 55, 75
  rorqual, 75
  sperm, 70, 75
Whale-headed stork, 52
Whippoorwill, 49
White rhinoceros, 45
White stork, 54
Whooper swan, 63
Wildebeeste, 55
Wolf, 62, 85
Wood ant, 38
Woodpecker, 27
Woodpecker finch, 17
Worm, 12
Wrasse, ocellated, 40

Z

Zebra, 71, 76